Everybody's House — The Schoolhouse

With **Marilyn Curry**

Everybody's House — The Schoolhouse

Best Techniques for Connecting Home, School, and Community

Carolyn Warner

CORWIN PRESS, INC.
A Sage Publications Company
Thousand Oaks, California

For information address:

Corwin Press, Inc.
A Sage Publications Company
2455 Teller Road
Thousand Oaks, California 91320
e-mail: order@corwin.sagepub.com

SAGE Publications Ltd.
6 Bonhill Street
London EC2A 4PU
United Kingdom

SAGE Publications India Pvt. Ltd.
M-32 Market
Greater Kailash I
New Delhi 110 048 India

Printed in the United States of America

Library of Congress Cataloging-in-Publication Data

Warner, Carolyn.
    Everybody's house—the school house : best techniques for
connecting home, school, and community / author, Carolyn Warner.
        p.   cm.
    Includes bibliographical references.
    ISBN 0-8039-6482-X (pbk. : acid-free paper). — ISBN 0-8039-6485-4
(cloth : acid-free paper)
    1. Home and school—United States.   2. Education—Parent
participation—United States.   3. Community and school—United
States.   I. Title.
LC225.3.W37   1997
306.43—dc21   96-51309

This book is printed on acid-free paper.

01   10 9 8 7 6 5 4 3 2

Corwin Press Production Editor: S. Marlene Head
Editorial Assistant: Nicole Fountain
Typesetters: Rebecca Evans & Andrea D. Swanson
Cover Designer: Marcia R. Finlayson

Contents

Foreword

Show me a company that isn't involved with schools and education, and I'll show you a company that hasn't thought seriously about its future.

Show me an educator who thinks his or her school can "go it alone," and I'll show you a person who is out of touch with reality.

Show me a community that doesn't value its young people and their education, and I'll show you a ghost town in the making.

Show me a family that doesn't want its children to succeed in school, and I'll show you a family that needs help.

These are strong statements, but they point up a dramatic truth about the relationship between schools, families, businesses, and the communities in which they are all located: These institutions are utterly dependent upon one another for survival and success. However, understanding these realities and knowing exactly what to do about them are two completely different matters.

In truth, I know of very few business owners who do not understand that their future workforce, as well as their future customers, clients, and stockholders, can be found in the schools today. I also have met very few educational leaders who do not understand that government dollars alone cannot provide all that their schools need in order to succeed in their mission of giving as many young people as possible a quality basic education. I have never encountered a parent who expressed indifference about their children's future—but I have met many who were uncertain about their ability to do anything about it. And increasingly, communities and community leaders are coming to grips with the reality that the quality of their schools determines to a great extent the economic and social quality of life that determines what kind of place that community will be.

Our company, Metropolitan Life, has understood these realities for many years. We recognize that as a major American corporate institution, we have a direct responsibility to do what we can—when and where we can—to help build stronger families *and* better communities. We have come to recognize clearly that whenever we do something to help schools, educators, and communities, as well as young people and their families, we also make a statement about our faith in the future.

For these reasons, we believe that partnering with schools and educators is one of the best ways that any business entity can help ensure its own future well-being, in addition to the well-being of its employees and the communities in which they live. I believe that most businesses in American are coming to the same conclusion.

So the question for businesses more and more becomes, "How do we do it? How do we involve ourselves with schools in a manner that would be both helpful and productive?"

Educators, of course, must answer the other side of that question: "How do we reach out and involve the businesses in our community in mutually beneficial partnership with our schools?"

There is, however, an even more important question we all must answer: "How can schools and employers work together to help families become more involved in the education of their children?"

No thoughtful person believes that schools alone can do a complete job of educating a child. And clearly, we understand that employers cannot *mandate* that their employees be good, conscientious, involved parents.

So how *do* schools and their corporate partners work together to help families and communities become part of a positive educational partnership?

This is where *Everybody's House—The Schoolhouse* comes in. Carolyn Warner has been a prominent education and public policy leader, commentator, and advocate for many years. Her work is well known in both the business and educational communities. We at MetLife have worked with her to develop more and better ways for our company to become involved with schools. Because of Warner's long-standing advocacy—as a school board member, an elected official, a national-stature consultant, and a business-owner, herself—of the school-community-family-business partnership, she is uniquely qualified to write a book that provides countless insights and practical techniques on how these vital partnerships can be developed and strengthened.

To be effective, a book has to have both a perspective and a target audience.

Everybody's House is written from the perspective that it doesn't take secret formulas and magic to strengthen the involvement of families and communities with schools; what is required is an understanding of who your school community is and what their interests are and how knowledge of this key marketing data—to put it in business terminology—can be employed to increase the involvement of families and communities with schools.

Although Warner might just as easily have written the book with the business community as her target audience, she has—wisely, I believe—instead intended the book to be used first and primarily by educators.

There are two good reasons for this. First, because schools are the primary partnering target for employers and communities, it is appropriate that school leaders "take the point" in reaching out to develop these partnerships. Second, *Everybody's House* is a logical extension of Warner's earlier book, *Promoting Your School: Going Beyond PR*. Taken together, these two volumes provide educational leaders with the best "cookbooks" I have seen, to help them develop concrete plans, programs, and strategies to reach out to the greater community and involve all stakeholders in the process of building not only stronger schools but stronger families and neighborhoods.

I firmly believe that if every school leader in America adopted just one or two ideas from *Promoting Your School* and used the outreach strategies in *Everybody's House* to implement them, we would see dramatic improvement in the involvement of families with schools, schools with communities, and employers with their employees.

I believe this book is not only useful but important for another reason. Carolyn Warner recognizes the fact that there is no longer a simple definition of "family." America's families are like America's children: They come in all shapes, sizes, colors, and configurations. *Everybody's House* not only encourages us to recognize and understand this diversity, it points the way for using diversity as a quality of strength. In this regard, the message goes far beyond the schoolhouse door.

I am delighted to commend *Everybody's House—The Schoolhouse* to members of the education community. I commend it with equal enthusiasm to every other stakeholder in our schools, because this book's title encapsulates some great truths: Our schools are truly enterprises in which all of us have a stake; what goes on in our schools is of importance to all of us; our children are our future's only hope; and our involvement with *their* future is the most important responsibility any of us can meet.

Barbara Healy
National Marketing Director
MetLife Resources

Acknowledgments

The involvement strategies and program ideas mentioned throughout this book have come from a variety of sources and from all parts of the country. They are included because they have been successfully used at one or more schools. The ideas were shared by principals, teachers, and parents who practice inclusiveness and involvement—and who are excited about possibilities and opportunities. They all believe that schools and parents should jointly set high expectations and, together, can help students meet these standards.

Individual credit is not always given for three reasons: A number of the ideas were mentioned by more than one person, some suggestions were given verbally in group settings, and many contributors said their programs were not original but borrowed from another school or another educator. No one has a lock on good ideas and good programs; we find them everywhere. Acknowledging that imitation is the sincerest form of flattery, the educators with whom I have spoken and corresponded are eager to see their successful involvement programs adopted by others.

I extend my grateful appreciation and thanks to Marilyn Curry for her help in preparing this book and to the following contributors. If I have missed any contributors, I issue a blanket apology and a sincere "Thank you!"

Larry Alkire, Agua Fria High School, Avondale, Arizona
Fred Anderson,[1] Custer County High School, Miles City, Montana
Jeffrey L. Athey,[1] Dodgeville High School, Dodgeville, Wisconsin
Edward Bales, Motorola, Schaumberg, Illinois
Eddie Basha, Basha Foods, Chandler, Arizona

Thomas Blair,[1] Sauk Rapids High School, Sauk Rapids, Minnesota

David J. Bolger, Zephyr Communications, Scottsdale, Arizona

Jenell Bovis, Windy Ridge Elementary School,[2] Orlando, Florida

Thomas C. Bowers, Triton Elementary School, Bourbon, Indiana

Mary Bradford, MetLife Resources, Bethesda, Maryland

Barbara Clark, Motorola, Tempe, Arizona

Michael L. Cunningham,[1] Clendenin Middle School, Clenendin, West Virginia

Michelle Doyle, U.S. Department of Education, Washington, DC

Timothy J. Dyer, National Association of Secondary School Principals, Reston, Virginia

Sara Eggleston, Hazel S. Pattison Elementary School,[2] Katy, Texas

Barbara Ferraro, Rye Neck High School,[2] Mamaroneck, New York

Jim Findley, Westside High School,[2] Omaha, Nebraska

Constance W. Gall, Flower Mound Elementary School,[2] Flower Mound, Texas

John Gilbert,[1] Highland Oaks Middle School, North Miami Beach, Florida

Timothy C. Gilbert, Cope Middle School,[2] Bossier City, Louisiana

Larry Gregory,[1] Desert Hill Middle School, Kennewick, Washington

David Guel, Travis Middle School,[2] McAllen, Texas

Kay Harmless, Green Elementary School, Allen, Texas

Merle P. Herndon, Linkhorne Elementary School,[2] Lynchburg, Virginia

Richard Janezich,[1] Brooklyn Center High School, Brooklyn Center, Minnesota

Mary Grace Jarvis,[3] Smoky Hill High School, Aurora, Colorado

Arline Kalishman, A. B. Green Middle School,[2] Richmond Heights, Missouri

Jeffrey L. Kane, Forest Meadow Junior High School,[2] Dallas, Texas

Jennifer Killian, Grapevine High School, Grapevine, Texas

Karen Kleinz, Kleinz Communications, Peoria, Arizona

Thomas Koerner, National Association of Secondary School Principals, Reston, Virginia

Milton Kuykendall,[1] Horn Lake High School, Horn Lake, Mississippi

Sharon Lewis, Simpson Elementary School, Phoenix, Arizona

Linda Lisciarelli, community activist, Phoenix, Arizona

Lisa Lisciarelli, Apple Computers, Tempe, Arizona

Tom Lorig, Motorola, Mesa, Arizona

Norma Malamud, Alahambra Elementary School District, Phoenix, Arizona

Catherine McKee, Motorola, Scottsdale, Arizona

Larry Myatt, Fenway Middle College High School,[4] Boston, Massachussetts

Linda Nathan, Fenway Middle College High School,[4] Boston, Massachusetts

Donna Neill, community activist, Phoenix, Arizona

Teacola Offutt, Orchard School of Science,[2] Cleveland, Ohio

William Patterson, Mirage Elementary School, Glendale, Arizona

Donna Peterson, North Star Elementary School,[2] Nikiski, Alaska

Darlene Pierce, American Association of School Administrators, Arlington, Virginia

Lee E. Robert, Cavett Robert Communications, Phoenix, Arizona

Julianne C. Robertson, Oak Elementary School,[2] Bartlett, Tennessee

Laura Roth, Corporate//Education Consulting Inc., Phoenix, Arizona

Barbara Russell, Memphis City Schools, Memphis, Tennessee

Perry Sandler,[1] Joseph Pulitzer Intermediate School 145, Jackson Heights, New York

Patrick E. Savini, Sussex Technical High School,[2] Georgetown, Delaware

Jane Schuck, Dakota Meadows Middle School,[2] North Mankato, Minnesota

Phillip R. Silsby,[1] Belleville West High School, Belleville, Illinois

Adrienne Smith, Jobs for America's Graduates, Alexandria, Virginia

Janice Sorsby, Balmoral Elementary School, Memphis, Tennessee

Pamela Stanfield, Westchester Elementary School, Kirkwood, Missouri

Sandy Steffens, Village Meadows Elementary School, Phoenix, Arizona

George Stone, Seaford Middle School,[2] Seaford, Delaware

George V. Tignor,[3] Parsons High School, Parsons, Kansas

Susan Van Zant, Morning Creek Elementary School,[2] San Diego, California

Alan M. Veach,[1] McNeil High School, Austin, Texas (now at Conroe High School, Conroe, Texas)

George V. Voinovich, Governor of Ohio, Columbus, Ohio

Thomas F. Wilson, Eagan High School,[2] Eagan, Minnesota

Jennifer Winter, Corporate//Education Consulting, Inc., Phoenix, Arizona

Joseph S. Wojtena,[1] Champaign Central High School, Champaign, Illinois

Joan B. Wright,[1] Wenatchee High School,[2] Wenatchee, Washington

Notes

1. State Principal of the Year.

2. Blue Ribbon School, U.S. Department of Education.

3. National Principal of the Year.

4. New American High School, U.S. Department of Education, and the National Council for Research in Vocational Education.

About the Author

Carolyn Warner has gained national stature as one of America's most articulate educational and public policy leaders. A speaker and seminar leader of uncommon skill, she averages more than 70 presentations each year to education, government, and corporate groups nationwide.

Formerly State Superintendent of Public Instruction in Arizona, the first noneducator to hold the post, Warner was reelected twice and served for a total of 12 years. Quickly developing a reputation for advocating educational accountability (both fiscal and academic) and citizen participation in educational decision making, she was also noted for her leadership in integrating vocational and academic skills among Arizona's students.

In 1996, she received both the Distinguished Service Award from the National Association of Secondary School Principals (NAASP) and the National Policy Leader of the Year Award from the National Association of State Boards of Education (NASBE).

Drawing on her vast experience in government, education, and communications, Warner heads her own firm, Corporate//Education Consulting Inc., which offers consulting, seminar, training, and lecture services. She is the author of two books and numerous articles.

Introduction

Wherever and whenever in this nation I talk to educational leaders, the most frequent question I get is, "Carolyn, how can we possibly do everything that is expected of us with the resources we have?"

My answer is, "You can't." We expect so much of our schools today that it is literally impossible for them to do everything they are asked to do. We compound this by also expecting that they will not fail—ever! Clearly, no business would ever set such standards for itself. Yet this is what we ask of our schools.

Given this reality, what can schools do to meet society's expectations?

I am convinced that schools must, like never before, reach out: reach out to families, to the community, and to the private sector. Schools must enlist every one of these constituencies in the educating, and in the educational, process. And they must do it in an overt, organized, systematic way. It is too important to be left to chance or whim.

Each of these varied constituencies has a similar responsibility: They must recognize and embrace the fact that if they want schools to succeed, they must do their part to help them. Parents must become more involved in the education of their children. (In this book, the words *parent* and *family* are used interchangeably.) The community must become more involved with its schools. And the private sector must recognize that it bears a unique responsibility, and has the unique opportunity, to directly determine the quality and the capability of its future labor force.

But it is not enough that these stakeholders simply recognize their responsibilities. What must happen is that they to move beyond recognition to action. This converting of recognition into action is the responsibility of school leaders who genuinely seek to involve families, communities, and employers with their schools. Providing practical, tactical, and strategic assistance to those educational leaders who are willing to accept this challenge is what this book is all about.

One of the most encouraging signs in American education today is the extent to which educators all across America are accepting this involvement challenge. Leaders in schools and school districts—large and small; rural, urban, and suburban; rich and poor—are devising and implementing strategies to generate involvement. Some of these strategies are simple; some are complex. But those that are successful all have some elements in common: They are tailored to the particular demographic, social, and economic characteristics of their school communities; and they all have school leaders who are determined to reach out and bring families, communities, and employers into the equation of educational success.

Recognizing that good ideas are truly everywhere, we contacted a number of outstanding educators, including state Principals of the Year and principals of Blue Ribbon Schools, and we asked them for their most successful techniques for involving their external constituencies. We also asked them how the demographics of their schools affected the strategies they employed. I am grateful beyond measure to the dozens of principals and other educators who shared their thoughts, ideas, challenges, and strategies with us. This is a book that reflects, to the greatest possible degree, the thinking and the action of these educational leaders.

In my earlier book, *Promoting Your School—Going Beyond PR,* I addressed the many techniques that schools might use to communicate with their various constituencies. This book, *Everybody's House,* focuses on the techniques and strategies that can be successfully employed for seeking and gaining the involvement of those constituencies. Taken together, they provide educational practitioners with an overall framework for both reaching out and then bringing in these stakeholders.

I am convinced that most families, most communities, and most employers want to be part of the solution to the challenges that confront our schools, not part of the problem. But very often, they do not know how. This book is intended to help educators adopt, adapt, and implement programs that show these stakeholders how to be a part of that solution.

Carolyn Warner

A Note About Involvement Evaluations

At the end of each chapter there is an involvement evaluation section that corresponds to the thrust of that chapter. These evaluations are intended to be thought provokers and idea stimulators rather than "tests" or time-consuming research projects.

The involvement evaluations can be used by a teacher or education professional in evaluating a class or a program, as well as by a principal in evaluating the school. Obviously, the same approach could be used in evaluating an entire school district.

Once you have reviewed and completed any of the evaluations, you may wish to then develop a communications plan and materials to help reach a particular group of stakeholders or a particular audience.

In *Promoting Your School—Going Beyond PR* (also published by Corwin Press), there are many copy-ready examples of news releases, survey forms, contact forms, newsletter formats, and other tools to support outreach efforts at every level.

1 Connecting Home and School

*Parent and Family Involvement
and Student Success*

Why Parent and Family Involvement Is Important

I have never met a parent who wanted his or her child to fail. However, some parents just don't know how to help their child succeed. Schools *do* know how to help a child succeed. And they know that children succeed best when the home and school are partners.

As the millennium approaches, much is being said and written about our society's "disconnectedness." The more we hear about the breakdown of the American family, the increasing violence on our streets and in our schools, and the decline of shared community values, the more we realize how dependent we are on the teaching and support provided by our nation's social foundations of school and home. Our democracy has survived and thrived on the fundamental belief in the importance of an educated populace.

One of the most essential things a parent can instill in a child is the importance of education. If a parent shows no interest in the child's school or what the child is learning, the message given to that child is that education is not important. And it is difficult, often impossible, for schools to counter such a negative message. We've all read about the high motivation and academic success of many students from Asian countries. There is little dispute that a major factor in that success is the high priority their families place on education.

Evidence shows unequivocally that school programs that emphasize parent involvement, and schools that relate well to their communities, have students who outperform those in schools lacking these qualities. And the benefits of involvement are as diverse as the families and schools themselves. Not only do students flourish, but schools clearly are strengthened when parents take an active interest in their children's education. The results include better attendance, improved behavior, a higher quality of education, and a safe, disciplined learning environment.

> The network created when families and school work together is critical to the maturation and control of students. When caring is expressed between home and the school, the child feels more secure and performs and behaves better. (Principal George Stone, Seaford Middle School, Delaware)

Thirty years of educational research (as well as our own experience and common sense) tell us that parental involvement in a child's education is the most consistent indicator of whether that child is successful in school. Controllable home factors such as student absenteeism, the variety and availability of reading materials in the home, and frequency of television viewing account for almost all the differences in average student achievement.[1]

Statistics on earning potential also serve to underscore the value of family involvement. A 1994 U.S. Census Bureau study reveals that a difference in lifetime earnings between a high school dropout and a college graduate is close to $1 million.[2]

Studies of individual families show that family attitudes and actions are more important to student success than family income or education. For example, one of the most important activities for building the knowledge required for eventual reading success is reading aloud to children and listening to them read.

Today's effective educators find ways to bridge the gap between home and school and to increase involvement of parents and family members in creating this essential foundation of support.

Building a "Connectiveness" With Children

If children need both parents and educators to realize their potential, parents and teachers must strive to build a "connectiveness" for children by

- Working together to be successful in their respective roles
- Developing a relationship of mutual trust and respect that transcends cultural, social, and language barriers

- Expanding opportunities for interaction and giving parents a voice in decision making
- Promoting lifelong learning as a key to success

Involvement Helps Get Bond Elections Passed

When we are reminded that only one fourth of American households have school-age children in them, we know that community involvement beyond families with children is essential to the well-being of education. In numbers alone, families who have a strong stake in the quality of schools are outnumbered by those who don't. Among the "don'ts" are those who aren't the least bit interested in education, those who don't think they should have to spend their tax dollars on other people's children, and, increasingly, those who are hostile to public education.

By involving and assisting parents and families, we encourage them to become advocates for the school with the general public, thereby increasing the school's chances of success in bond issues and finance elections and in building overall support for public education.

> Support for positive budget notes and bonds from the community has increased as a result of creating a community school. Senior citizens are regular participants in our school as volunteers and as learners, and parents have access to school resources through our College/Career Center. (Principal Barbara Ferraro, Rye Neck High School, Mamaroneck, New York)

Involvement Helps Stabilize School Budgets

Educators today can ill afford not to involve families and community as local, state, and federal funding for public education continues to decrease and student enrollment continues to rise. These factors force schools to find different and economically efficient ways to operate, including increasing not only class size but the size of campuses as well. As districts seek to stretch their capital funding dollars, K-6 elementary schools for 900-plus students are now becoming commonplace and no longer exceptions in public school systems across the country. In spite of their best efforts, without volunteer help, educators cannot begin to address the individual needs of students in such large campus environments or in the challenging atmosphere of urban schools.

Visitors are impressed by the enormous staff available to meet the needs of students at North Star. What they may not realize is that on any given day, 20% of this staff is made up of volunteers. That's all day—every day! This past year over 7,000 volunteer hours were logged at the school, equal to six full-time staff members. What a positive difference this makes in the lives of our students. (Principal Donna Peterson, North Star Elementary School, Nikiski, Alaska)

The parent involvement at North Star is impressive any way you look at it. But this Alaskan community is unique in that many families are employed by the oil industry and work a rotational schedule of 1 week on and 1 week off. Others are employed in the commercial fishing industry, which means that they have the winter months free. North Star's flexible policy in accommodating work schedules has resulted in a large and diverse base of volunteers from which to draw.

Our volunteer program is called P.I.P. (Patrons Involvement Program). We use the word *patrons* instead of *parents* because we have so many grandparent and community volunteers. We have them sign in and sign out, giving the time they arrive and leave, so that we can keep track of volunteer hours. At the end of the year, we publicize the number of hours donated and the value of this "in-kind" contribution. We figure that if we had to pay an employee for that same work, the cost, including benefits, would be roughly $10.00 an hour. So if 2,500 hours are donated, the school has saved $25,000—and that $25,000 can be spent elsewhere. (Principal Thomas Bowers, Triton Elementary School, Bourbon, Indiana)

What Is Involvement?

Involvement is a broad term and doesn't necessarily mean that one or both parents have to volunteer at school once a week, once a month, or once a year. Of course, it could mean that. Or it could mean that involvement in their child's education takes place at home—and occasional visits to school occur because of the obligatory parent-teacher conference, to see their child perform, to watch a sporting event, or for Open House.

If parents only go to their child's school for conferences, performances, or sports, educators don't really complain. That's more than many parents do. We all recognize that parents are busy people and have the same obligations and stresses as the rest of us do. Still, we want to encourage involvement beyond the minimum. Educators must seek out parents who would be willing to volunteer their time and talents in ways that assist teachers and staff to help students and in ways that produce school programs and events that would not happen otherwise.

Schools have always encouraged parents' at-home interest and involvement in a child's education and welfare—from reading to young children, to teaching them moral values, monitoring what they watch on TV, and helping them with homework.

Parents who play an active role in their children's education, both at home and on campus as part of the school team, are able to maximize the many learning opportunities available and ensure a successful educational experience for their children. Parents who are advocates for their children ensure that they receive the best education the school has to offer. And to become effective advocates, parents must be knowledgeable about the school, its programs, and its needs, in addition to the specific educational needs of their own children.

Following are two examples of involvement, one emphasizing at-home involvement and one emphasizing in-school involvement. These cases aren't typical (perhaps, even extreme), but they are true, and they illustrate possibilities.

At-Home Support: Connecting With Parents

In some school attendance areas, just about all adults in a household work, so there is virtually no potential pool of in-school volunteers. Following is the story of how a school in such a neighborhood got that much-needed at-home support for its students.

This Grade 7-8 middle school is located in a suburban, middle-to-lower-income neighborhood. The suburb, bordering a large midwestern city, is where families move if they are able to leave the inner city. The school is composed of 38% minority students, and 75% of the students are on free or reduced lunch.

The junior high in question had a notorious reputation in the community, and any parents who could afford it would send their children to parochial or private school. For a student body of 200, the police came to the school over 300 times the previous year. Test scores were 46% below state average, and 20% of the seventh graders had failed every subject the year before. This was a school that had to be turned around!

A new principal was hired. But before she would accept the job, she insisted on a few conditions: one, that the district back her in her attempts to improve the school; two, that the junior high exchange buildings with an adjacent elementary school (the only changes to the elementary building involved enlarging restroom facilities and raising drinking fountains); and, three, that the entire school be repainted.

The incoming principal met with the faculty in May to lay out plans for the coming year. During the summer, all but three teachers resigned (and two of them left during that next school year). Because of budget constraints, most of the new teachers hired were right out of college. (It was already July, and these teachers were eager for a job.) A 3-day summer retreat was held in August to enable the new teachers to get acquainted and to inform them of plans for the coming school year. The principal had the support of the district, and at the retreat she was able to gain the support of the new teachers.

Parent and community support was needed. But it had to be at-home support because almost all the parents worked. Before school opened, a series of small meetings was held with a mix of teachers, parents, and community leaders in attendance. The purpose of those meetings was to articulate the visions that these groups had for the school and to come up with a mission statement. The summary of their vision and their mission statement became their motto: "All Students Will Succeed!"

One of the first tasks was to address the problem of those 20% failing seventh-grade students. It was determined that if they repeated seventh grade, the school atmosphere would be chaotic. So the students and their parents were informed that if the student signed a contract, he or she would pass conditionally to eighth grade. The contract conditions specified that the student would agree to be tutored for an hour after school each day and then take and pass the seventh-grade test in January. All failing students signed the contract. The district provided an extra bus so that these youngsters could be transported home later than usual.

The tutoring began—and the school turned around. The principal credits that individual and small-group tutoring as being the primary reason for the turnaround. Why? Because students began to realize that their teachers cared about them, wanted them to learn, and were concerned about their progress and willing to spend extra time to help them improve.

In the students' past experience, if they received a grade of D or F, they advanced sooner or later to the next grade anyway, but with little increased knowledge or level of understanding. The parents knew this (many had experienced it themselves) and knew that going on to a higher grade level without learning anything leads to dropping out, and being a dropout means their children's future prospects would be slim, indeed. This after-school tutoring caused both students and parents to realize how dedicated the teachers were. And because the teachers were trying harder, the students began trying harder—and the parents were witness to all of this.

At this school, no Ds or Fs are given, only A, B, C, and NQY (not quality yet). Lessons are studied until a student scores 70% or better on the material. (Remember their motto: "All Students Will Succeed!") To accomplish this, tutoring was absolutely necessary. Tutoring takes time, energy, dedication, and commitment—from students and teachers alike. There are no remedial or special education classes in this school. A student attends regular classes, and if he or she is falling behind, the student is tutored by the appropriate teacher after school.

One girl, 2 years older and quite a bit larger than her classmates, was one of the seventh-grade failures who signed a contract to go on to eighth grade. She had never experienced any success in school. After being in the tutoring program, she not only passed officially into eighth grade but made the honor roll. After "floating" through the graduation ceremony, she told one (actually several) of her teachers, "I never knew I could do it, and now I can graduate from high school. I can be somebody."

Even though there is gang activity in the neighborhood and gang members attend this school, there is no gang activity in the school. The principal lets the students know that what they do outside of school is their business and their parents' business, but what they do at school, and anywhere on school grounds, is her business and the teachers' business and the staff's business—and they will not tolerate any type of gang activity, including wearing gang colors. The students have accepted this and don't object. In fact, they seem to be grateful. They feel safe at school.

These junior high students are proud of their school. There is no graffiti on the newly painted, cream-colored walls. They don't misbehave in certain ways because it is not allowed. The consequences are immediate and the punishment well known.

If a students fights, it's an automatic 5-day suspension. If the student had been warned ahead of time and still fights, it's a 10-day suspension. The district administration and the parents support the principal on discipline policies. The parents want a safe environment for their children and they support a school that provides that safety. If parents have to be contacted, the call is made to their work; the ones who have night jobs (and this is a good many) are called at home. If a parent cannot be contacted any other way, a registered letter is sent.

Also not tolerated is being disrespectful to adults. In fact, politeness is demanded. Good behavior and academic progress are both rewarded. Food is a big motivator. Candy bars, apples, ice cream treats, and soft drinks are given out for rewards at every opportunity, including during the break between tests at the all-day, state-required testing. Points are accumulated so students can earn their way into certain activities, such as a monthly pizza party.

Who pays for the pizza and all the other goodies? The principal has a fund for such extras. Over the years, this money has come from a variety of sources, including state and foundation grants and corporate and business donations. This principal applies for grants whenever and wherever she can find them. Her superintendent knows that if a grant application comes to the district office, this principal wants to have the opportunity to look it over and apply for it.

A Student Advisory Group, made up of one student from each homeroom, meets by grade level with the principal once a week for 25 minutes during their advisory/homeroom period. They meet each week so that every child in the school gets a chance to participate in the advisory group. Soda pop and a bag of chips are passed around when the students arrive and they drink and munch throughout the meeting. Concerns of the students are discussed, and the principal is able to find out early on about potential problems that might affect the entire school and to explain directly to students why things are done as they are. This Student Advisory Group is an opportunity for strong two-way communication and enables the principal to keep her finger on the pulse of the school.

Student recommendations and suggestions are sincerely solicited. Two requests that keep coming up year after year, always at the beginning of school are, "Why can't we have a longer lunch period?" and "Why can't we have 15 minutes to change classes?" The principal says, "Fine, let's do it. But first we'll have to lengthen the school day because the state mandates that you have to spend X number of hours in school each day." Because students don't want to exchange a longer lunch or passing period for a longer day, that takes care of that.

When a Blue Ribbon School evaluator came from Washington, D.C., she selected students at random and asked them what they liked about the school. Some of the responses were, "Our teachers care about us," "We don't have to be afraid here," "Everybody's nice to each other," and "The school is clean."

When the evaluator asked about graffiti or whether they had ever seen anyone with a weapon or drugs at school, the responses were, "No, we're not allowed to write on the walls," "No, we're not allowed to bring weapons to school," and "No, we're not allowed to have drugs at school."

The "we're not allowed to" phrase turned up again and again. The students with whom the evaluator spoke all clearly understood that certain behavior was unacceptable—and this didn't seem to bother them in the least. If rules are clear and infractions are met with swift and reasonable punishment that is fairly meted out, students accept this, as do parents.

An incident of this nontolerance for showing disrespect to adults is exemplified in the episode of an eighth-grade student who had been selected queen of the school's prom. On the day of the dance, the girl was passing the office and saw a woman with whom she had previously had neighborhood trouble waiting in the outer office. The soon-to-be-former prom queen stuck her head in the office and made an ugly remark to the woman. The remark was overheard by the principal, who promptly suspended the girl, which meant she wouldn't be allowed to attend the dance. But it didn't turn out to be a major school "incident" because everybody knew the rules—the girl, the other students, the teachers, her parents, the district administrators—and knew that there was zero tolerance for rudeness and disrespect in that school (A.B. Green Middle School, Richmond Heights, Missouri).

In-School Involvement: Connecting With Students

The setting for this illustration is an upper-income, suburban high school, and the program is a Youth Employment Service that was originated, organized, and run by parents.

The initial reaction by many in the school and community was that these students (most were from wealthy families) weren't interested in getting jobs. However, when the employment service was announced, the positive response from the students was overwhelming. Parents (i.e., mothers, in this instance), with a closet-size office in the school, got the program off the ground by notifying students about the employment service and accepting applications.

Meanwhile, other mothers went into the community, signing up employers who were willing to offer part-time, weekend, or summer jobs. As the program progressed, dads became involved in the job search part of the program. The jobs obtained included typical part-time work such as office receptionist, cleaning garages, baby-sitting, retail sales, yard work, and restaurant jobs.

One of the mothers trained a number of students to serve at private dinner parties by teaching them how to properly set and clear a table, wash dishes, clean up, and perform other busing chores. This service was in much demand, and the organizers were surprised at the number of teens willing to work on Thanksgiving, Christmas, and other holidays. Another mother trained students in baby-sitting skills. The salaries of both baby-sitters and servers were set by the employment service; all other salaries were set by the employers.

Volunteers staffed the employment office during school hours every day and would always check by telephone with employers to determine how the student employees were doing—Did they get to work on time? Were they absent much? and so on. They also solicited feedback from the students as to how they were treated by employers. Records were kept for handy reference on both employers and employees.

These parent volunteers gained the respect of the entire student body and were often visited during the day by students who wanted to talk about jobs, careers, SAT scores, college, peer pressure, and just about anything else teens like to talk about. The parents did not act as counselors but lent a willing ear to any student who wanted to chat.

This employment service required quite a number of volunteers, and as the program evolved, it was determined that those parents who remained active did so because they were able to work in areas in which they felt most comfortable, they saw that their efforts were making a difference in young lives, and they had the support of school faculty and staff.

The Youth Employment Service is still active 23 years later—but now the office is larger and air-conditioned (Clayton High School, Missouri).

Do Parents Want to Get Involved?

Research shows us that there is public support for greater family involvement in learning.

- 40% of parents across the country do not think they are devoting enough time and attention to their children's education.[3]
- 89% of company executives feel that the biggest obstacle to school reform is a lack of parental involvement.[4]
- 72% of students aged 10-13 would like to talk to their parents more about schoolwork; 48% of older adolescents, aged 14-17, felt likewise.[5]

The National Education Goals, as set out in the Goals 2000: Educate America Act, express the desires and needs of Americans for improvement in education over the next several years. In 1989, America's governors and the president met and developed the original six goals, and the U.S. Congress with a strong bipartisan vote added two new goals. Since then, these goals have been recognized by every major group of parents, educators, and business people.

The Parental Participation Goal (Goal 8) states: "By the year 2000, every school will promote partnerships that will increase parental involvement and participation in promoting the social, emotional, and academic growth of children."

The media is constantly telling us how important, actually, how vital, it is for parents to be involved in their children's education. A national awareness has been raised and conscientious parents have responded. There are new programs and revitalized programs in schools all across the country that have attracted active parent and family involvement. Whether groups are affiliated with the PTA or the PTO, whether the group is a formally organized local organization or just a parent helping a teacher, involvement and volunteerism is the wave of the future.

There is an incredible untapped resource of people within local communities willing to lend their time and expertise in helping schools and children. It is no longer a question of whether educators should invite them to join the school team, it is only a question of when—and the sooner the better.

Do Educators Really Want Parents Involved?

Teachers rank increasing the involvement of parents in their children's education as the top priority goal for educators over the next few years.[6]

A 1996 poll of 802 elementary and middle school principals, conducted by the National Association of Elementary School Principals (NAESP), reveals their top five priorities:[7]

- Motivating students (97%)
- Involving parents in their children's schoolwork (94%)
- Accommodating and paying for increasing numbers of special education children (93%)
- Keeping up with education technology (93%)

- Accepting and getting staff to accept additional social responsibilities that once belonged in the home, such as good manners and honesty (91%)

By contrast, these principals worried less about some of the hot media issues: competing with private, for-profit companies (32%); sharing decision-making authority with parents and community (50%); and handling local pressures for school choice, vouchers, and charter schools (49%).

Fads come and go in education. It's popular now for educators to say they actively solicit volunteers; that parents, grandparents, neighbors, and members of the community at large are welcome to come to school anytime. But saying it and meaning it are two different things—and *actually doing it* is something else again.

Not all principals and teachers welcome volunteers. In fact, if the truth be told, many don't. (And never, ever put a volunteer with a faculty or staff member who does not want one.) Educators have so much to do already that the time and organization it takes to train an effective volunteer, or just to have something planned for them to do when they come in on a regular basis, may be an overwhelming task.

> Getting parents involved in PTA and other "parent nights" is a major problem for us. We often spend many hours of planning and organizing without much return (i.e., parents in attendance). (Texas principal, K-5 elementary school)

There is no denying that trying to get parents involved means an increased time commitment and, perhaps, discouragement. Outreach efforts have to be constant and continuing and *creative.* An invitation in the school newsletter or a flyer brought home by a child will do it for a few parents, but not for most. And, of course, you will always have those few parents (mostly mothers) who help a great deal and stay involved with all aspects of the school.

Sometimes principals and teachers decide the results are just not worth the effort. Intentions may have been good at one time, but past experiences were negative. You have to accept the fact that unintended consequences are bound to occur. Perhaps you will have to mediate personality conflicts between group members. Or you may have to be on guard against a clique forming that won't be open and welcoming to new volunteers.

One of the things that often holds educators back is the fear of what they will have to give up with increased parent involvement, things such as autonomous control of agendas and speedy decision making.

But schools that have made the extra effort, a sincere effort, to involve family and community members say the results are worth it. It immediately helps students, and it pays off in dividends down the road when you need advocates for a new program, votes for a bond election or levy, or support for the school in a crisis.

Educators at Champaign Central High School, Illinois have identified the following reasons why they continue to make that extra effort to involve parents, family, and community:

- To enhance the sense of pride in community and school
- To enlist powerful allies in parents when dealing with difficult students and situations
- To increase financial support for schools (bond issues, private sector funding, funding for activities)
- To convince parents to "buy into" and not sabotage educational decisions
- To improve educational opportunities for students

At one point I entered a school where the parents were not supportive. After several years, they were the "best"—and it was a fantastic experience. I've since left that school, but what a great memory I have of those parents and that school. (Iowa principal, K-6 elementary school)

Qualities Shared by Educators Who Successfully Involve Parents

In their book *Parents On Your Side*,[8] Lee and Marlene Canter describe four qualities shared by teachers who have been effective in involving parents in the educational process.

1. They know they must have the support of parents.
2. In every interaction with parents, they demonstrate their concern for the child.
3. In all situations, they treat parents the way they want to be treated.
4. In every interaction with parents, they demonstrate professionalism and confidence.

These qualities apply to all staff members—and not just at the building level. They also apply to central office administrators and staff—and not just in dealings with parents, but also with employees. Just as we model appropriate behaviors for students, we need to model them for staff and parents as well.

Changing an American Institution

According to anthropologist Margaret Mead, "We are now at a point where we must educate our children in what no one knew yesterday, and prepare our schools for what no one knows yet."[9]

Breaking Ranks: Changing an American Institution, a study from the National Association of Secondary School Principals (NASSP) on improving the American high school for the 21st century, states:

> A high school builds its success on a series of strong and positive relationships with and among those both inside and outside the building. These relationships start with the ways in which teachers, students, and others in the school relate to each other and continue through the links that the school forms with parents, public officials, community agencies, business representatives, neighboring schools, and others on the outside.[10]

To forge these outside links, the NASSP report recommends that the high school of the 21st century

1. Regard itself as a community in which members of the staff collaborate to develop and implement the school's learning goals
2. Engage students' families as partners in the students' education
3. Help coordinate, in conjunction with agencies in the community, the delivery of health and social services for youths
4. Develop political and financial relationships with individuals and organizations in the community to foster ongoing support for educational programs and policies
5. Foster productive business partnerships that support and supplement educational programs
6. Form partnerships with agencies for youths that support and supplement the regular programs of the schools
7. Require each student to participate in a service program in the community or in the school itself that has educational value

Notes

1. P. E. Barton and R. J. Coley, *America's smallest school: The family*. Princeton, NJ: Educational Testing Service, 1992.

2. U.S. Bureau of the Census, *Educational attainment in the United States: March 1993 and 1992*. Washington, DC: Government Printing Office, 1994.

3. P. Finney, "The PTA/Newsweek National Education Survey." *Newsweek*, May 17, 1993.

4. N. Perry, "School reform: Big pain, little gain." *Fortune* 128, November 29, 1993.

5. National Commission on Children, *Speaking of kids: A national survey of children and parents*. Washington, DC: Author, 1991.

6. Louis Harris and Associates, *Metropolitan Life survey of the American teacher 1993: Violence in American public schools*. New York: Author, 1993.

7. Fax news service of the National School Public Relations Association, March 22, 1996.

8. Lee Canter and Marlene Canter, *Parents on your side*. Santa Monica, CA: Lee Canter & Associates, 1991.

9. Quoted in Carolyn Warner, *The last word: A treasury of women's quotes*. Englewood Cliffs, NJ: Prentice Hall, 1993.

10. *Breaking ranks: Changing an American institution*. A report of the National Association of Secondary School Principals in partnership with the Carnegie Foundation for the Advancement of Teaching. Reston, VA: National Association of Secondary School Principals, 1996.

Involvement Evaluation

1. Does your district have a policy or a goals statement on involvement? If so, do you follow it? Explain.

_____

_____

_____

_____

_____

2. How would increased parent involvement improve your school?

_____

_____

_____

_____

_____

3. List all the things you will have to give up or do differently to provide for volunteers.

_____

_____

_____

_____

_____

4. Give three reasons why you think there isn't more parent involvement in your school. How can you overcome each of these obstacles?

_____

_____

_____

_____

_____

5. Who initiates most of the involvement activities at your school?

Principal ____ Teachers ____ Staff ____ Parent organizations ____ Other ____

Which of these groups has been the most successful and why?

_____

_____

_____

_____

_____

2 Families of Today and Tomorrow: Who Are They?

Society's Changing Demographics

The "Good Old Days"

Our population is changing; our country is changing. We can never go back to what we think of as the "good old days," a time when life was simple. Of course, life has never been simple, so during those "good old days" people weren't aware that they were living in them. Maybe they were too busy reminiscing about the previous "good old days." Isn't it wonderful how time has a way of dulling unpleasant memories?

When schools were first established in this country, they served a rural, agricultural, and largely Protestant society. The curriculum was a body of lore to be passed on to the young of a relatively homogeneous society.

In examining that homogeneous society of yore more closely, however, we realize that it quickly became less and less homogeneous and more and more diverse. Children of the uneducated poor had little schooling; they were needed as workers to help support the family. African Americans were not allowed to participate in full citizenship or to have equal access to education or opportunity. A great influx of non-English-speaking, non-Protestant immigrants transformed our cities, and it was the job of schools to "Americanize" these immigrant children. Our earlier, rather homogeneous society didn't last long.[1]

The "New" America

What is the United States in store for as we approach the 21st century? In any discussion about families, we need to take a look at demographic trends and their likely effect on education.[2]

- The world's population is growing, but at a slower pace than previously. Fertility rates are declining, but a higher percentage of infants are surviving. Our planet is becoming more ethnically diverse and ethnically mixed, and much less white. Presently, 17% of Earth's 5.6 billion people are white; this number will decrease to 9% by the year 2015. Each year, 95% of the world's growth can be found in developing nations. The population of "haves" is diminishing, and the population of "have-nots" is increasing rapidly.

- In the United States, over 90% of the population growth is in the southern half of the nation. The northern population is older, richer, better educated, and declining in numbers. The white population is mostly concentrated in the north; the southern half is ethnically diverse, younger, poorer, and less well educated.

- U.S. immigration has reached record highs, but only 15% are from Europe. The other 85% of immigrants are from Mexico, Central and South America, and Asia. Whereas we were once a nation of blacks and whites, we are becoming a nation of the world. This will have a considerable effect because most of our common culture is European in origin. It is also important to note that so far, the new immigrants from non-European countries are doing as well as European immigrants have done in terms of educational access and economic progress.

- In 1993, 67% of children in U.S. schools were white; by the year 2030, most of America's school-age children will be minority—as will most Americans by the year 2050.[3]

- In 1993, one in three babies was born to a single mother. Half of the single mothers giving birth have never been married. Most single mothers are white, and 30% of single mothers are teenagers.

- Of the 14 million working poor, two thirds are women, the majority of whom have children under age 18. This means there is no one home to watch the kids after school. A 1993 study by the National Institute for Drug Abuse indicated that if a child is home alone for 10 hours a week, that child's risk of getting involved in dangerous drugs is doubled, regardless of ethnic background, household income, or location. After-school and summer programs for these children become a necessity, not a convenience.

- In 1994, 60% of women with children younger than age 6, and 57% of women with children younger than age 3, were in the labor force.[4]

- As of 1994, 5 million American children were living below the poverty line: 40% of the poor in the United States are children, and only 10% of the poor are elderly persons.

- By 2020, seniors will outnumber the school-age group for the first time in U.S. history. Children today are a precious and threatened resource and make up only 26% of our population.

- Only one household in four has a child in the public schools.

- Half of all marriages that took place in the 1970s and 1980s will end in divorce.

- The age group most likely to be the victim of violent crime in America is children aged 12-15.

- By the year 2000, more than 70% of the jobs in America will not require a college education.
- The average American adult can go an entire week without significant contact with a child under 18.

The Perfect American Family: Myth or Reality?

It is fascinating that in America we have created an icon of the perfect family: "Ozzie and Harriet," "Donna Reed," "Father Knows Best." In the 1950s, these TV shows depicted the way we perceived ourselves, the way we wanted to be (and to a large degree still want to be). Although most American families never looked like Donna Reed's, we like to think that they did. Thanks to the wonders of television, we did a wonderful job of marketing ourselves to ourselves.

The average American family has always had a more varied makeup than that pictured on TV. A *Phi Delta Kappan* special report on the family points out that not until the 1920s did even a majority of children come to live in a breadwinner-homemaker family. The Ozzie-and-Harriet model held sway for only 50 years, and at no time (even in the 1950s) did more than 60% of children live in such families for their entire childhood.[5]

What Public School Families Look Like

To give you an idea of the growing diversity in America's schools, here are how some of our nation's principals describe the families that make up their school communities:

Our school includes students from a rich diversity of cultural, ethnic, linguistic, and religious backgrounds. Thirty-two percent of our 846 students are non-Anglo. The largest ethnic group is Filipino; 173 students from 120 different families speak a language other than English in their homes. A large segment of these families is from Middle Eastern cultures. There are 22 different languages represented at our school. (California)

We are increasing in African American numbers, low-income numbers, and single-family numbers. We are providing more social services to meet their needs. (Delaware)

We have a very diverse school population. We have four emotionally handicapped classes, three trainable mentally handicapped classes, and one language and speech resource class. Of our regular education population, 25% come from inner-city minority; 25% from upper-middle-income neighborhoods, and 50% from a middle-income mix of single-family residences and apartments. We have many single-parent families, and 34% of students are on free and reduced lunch. (Florida)

Our community is extremely diverse. Families from South America and Europe join with the typical influx from our island neighbors, most notably, Cuba, Haiti, and Jamaica. (Florida)

We have more minorities, more low-socioeconomic-status students, and more single-parent families. This has shown a great increase in the last 6 to 7 years. (Illinois)

Special ed students were brought to the building against the will of the staff. It became a positive experience for incoming and current students and staff. Students became positively integrated and are an integral part of our school. I never thought it would work out that way. (Iowa)

Our school population is primarily middle-to-low income with an increasing number of at-risk students. There are increased numbers of students on welfare and from single-parent families. (Kansas)

We are an urban high school (250 students) located on the campus of a local community college. Our student body is 57% African American, 20% Caucasian; 19% have a primary language other than English (Spanish, Serbian, Portuguese, Haitian Creole, Russian, French, Polish, Vietnamese, Chinese, and three African dialects); 60% are on free or reduced lunch; 14% are teenage parents. We are a pilot program of the Boston City Schools. Classes are small, each teacher serves as an adviser to fewer than 20 students, and we have a strong school-to-career program. (Massachusetts)

Our community has been regarded as blue collar in the past, but we are in a transition phase now as more young professional families move in. (Minnesota)

Of the 800 students (Grades 7-12) enrolled, approximately 280 are open enrollments. Ownership and commitment to our school and our programs are primary concerns. (Minnesota)

Our community composition ranges from scientists at a state/federal research center to agricultural workers. Our school provides many more services that were once provided by families, churches, and other social organizations. We have a good many high school students who live as emancipated students. (Montana)

Thirty percent of our families are single-parent families. Middle- to upper-middle-income families make up the majority. Seventeen percent of students are on free and reduced lunches. We have added several programs for the at-risk students, including an alternative school and a directed studies program. (Nebraska)

We have many single parents, many non-English-speaking, lower-middle-class students from an urban neighborhood. Notices to parents are sent in English, Spanish, and Chinese, and we provide translators at meetings. (New York)

Our students are low income; most parents are not high school graduates; there is a 94% poverty rate. (Ohio)

Our students are middle class, one professional parent per household; most families are two-parent homes. A church-sponsored Children's Home also feeds into our school. Before- and after-school Y-Care is provided for working parents. (Tennessee)

Our school is 50% white and 50% black. All economic levels are represented, and it's difficult to promote understanding between all these levels. Sometimes I feel I'm trying to mix oil and water. As our minority enrollment increased, there were rumors about what this meant to our school and we had some white-flight. Those parents who have come back and spent time at our school are very positive and supportive and are surprised at how good our school is and how good an educational experience we offer. But how do we combat rumors? How do we get these parents back? (Texas)

We are composed mainly of upper-middle-class families. These families set very high academic standards. We have to find a way to meet their standards and teach children to achieve and meet goals without adding stress to their lives. We try to downplay competition among the children. It is important that these children be made aware of those less fortunate than themselves. (Texas)

Our school is along the border with Mexico and has a long tradition of two cultures. Of our 700 students, 10% are upper and middle class and the rest come from poor, local, and migrant families; 95% are Mexican American and about 50% have limited proficiency in English. (Texas)

In the past 10 years, our population has changed from a school with mostly stable, upper-middle-class families to a culturally rich mixture of ethnically and economically diverse students. Ten years ago we were surrounded by neighborhoods of single-family homes, but construction in the mid-1980s concentrated on apartments. As a result, we have 92 multifamily complexes in our attendance area. Additional increases in transient, economically disadvantaged, minority, non-English-speaking, and single-parent families are projected. Our population changed—so we changed. We confronted change with ingenuity and created new instructional methods and programs to help these students attain maximum success. (Texas)

Our city is small (60,000 in surrounding area) and has a rural and small city focus. Our school has a diverse economic, educational, social, and cultural mix. We have some students who live independently, and there is a day care program for students who have children of their own. (Washington)

We are a county seat community. While we live in a rural, midwestern setting, we are a cross between a town and a very small city. We have a number of students coming from farm families. Most students are white; we don't have much ethnic diversity. We have our share of single-parent families, grandparents serving as guardians, blended families, and students who live in foster homes. We have a difficult time getting parents of high school students in our building. Sometimes it appears that students don't wish their parents to be here (an image thing, it's not cool). We try to telephone parents more, make visitations, personally invite them to get more involved. (Wisconsin)

From east to west, it is obvious that our schools and communities continue to evolve, adding new and different pieces to the patchwork quilt of American life.

We cannot afford to create parent involvement programs that target only "ideal" families. Public schools have to work with families that exist right now, and if we are going to successfully reach them and involve them, we need to understand who they are.

Different Types of Families

Who are the families of today? They are as varied in structure as our students are in culture and ethnicity. Some of the more easily identified models include the following:

- *Traditional family:* married, breadwinner father and homemaker mother; some of these may be second marriages
- *Two-income family:* married, both parents work
- *Single-parent family:* divorced, never married, or single by choice
- *Blended family:* remarried with his/her/our children
- *Adoptive family:* married or single parents; can be multiethnic, multicultural, and/or special needs
- *Grandparents-as-parents family:* married or single, working or retired; caring for grandchildren temporarily or have full custody (this type of family is increasing)
- *Non-English-speaking family:* recent immigrants, may or may not be educated in their primary language
- *Foster family:* can be multiethnic, multicultural, and/or special needs; some children stay in foster care for a short time, some for years
- *Transient family:* married or single, migrant workers, homeless, unemployed
- *Same-sex-parents family*
- *Combined-household family:* several families living together, may or may not be related; may involve both parents, but usually does not

In 1955, 60% of American families reflected the breadwinner-homemaker and two-to-three children model. Thirty years later, fewer than 7% fit that description.[6]

Because change is inevitable, educators must recognize its earliest signs and prepare their programs accordingly. You might begin by finding out what percentage of your families fit into these different categories. Look at numbers for free and reduced lunch, collect information when registering students, get the information from teachers. Once you know what your specific family population looks like, you can develop an outreach program targeting these different types of families.

Some words of wisdom come from Dr. George Stone, principal of Seaford Middle School, Delaware: "Successful strategies for involving parents demonstrate caring, concern, communication, conferencing, and appointments to committees. It doesn't matter. All families need the same kinds of involvement."

What Makes Parent Involvement Work

Education researcher Benjamin Bloom has identified five factors found in successful parent involvement programs.[7]

1. *Climate.* Parents and visitors are made to feel welcome and treated with courtesy and respect. This starts with signs on the school campus and buildings, the friendliness of faculty and staff, the neat appearance of the campus, the "customer service" attitude.
2. *Relevance.* There is a focus on improving relationships, making volunteer work meaningful, providing help in parenting skills, homework with a purpose.
3. *Convenience.* Successful programs make it easy for parents to get involved. They provide transportation, child care, convenient scheduling.
4. *Communication.* Different methods of publicity are used, including school newsletters, church announcements, posters in stores, coffee klatches, key communicators, technology.
5. *Commitment.* The staff makes parent involvement a goal and are determined to make it work.

Reaching Out to Different Families

A growing body of research and literature convinces us that family involvement in children's learning is critical to their doing well in school and getting a good start in life. And studies also show that parents are interested in becoming involved in their children's schooling.

But it is a giant step between interest and action—and convincing parents to become involved is not always easy. In fact, it's a challenge. We can't force them, we can only offer them the opportunity. And it is up to teachers and principals to find creative ways to reach parents so that they will know about the involvement opportunities available both at home and at school.

Involvement Strategies for Different Types of Families

Following is a summary of ideas from educators around the country who have creatively and successfully targeted specific types of families.

Traditional Family

These are the easiest to reach; newsletter notices or teacher requests may be all that is needed. The family has usually made a conscious decision (because they can afford it) for the mother to stay home for the purpose of raising the children and being more involved in their activities.

If there are also preschoolers in the family, that cuts down on the mother's availability considerably. Several schools with active parent groups have been able to provide a room at school for child care on certain days for mothers who want to volunteer. This room has toys, paper, crayons, and so on and is staffed by volunteers.

Two-Income Family

Family time for working parents is at a premium. Most parents want to do right by their children, but in a society where most everyone works, parents are often pressed for time or just plain too tired to work with their children or to volunteer at school. With these parents, you must be aware of their time and energy limitations and be flexible in what you expect from them.

One study showed that the average mother spends less than half an hour a day talking or reading to her children, and the average father spends less than 15 minutes.

Still, don't always assume that because parents work they are completely unavailable to volunteer. Some jobs are part-time, some people (particularly mothers) job share, and more and more people today are working out of their homes and are able to make their own work schedule.

Enlightened companies will sometimes allow an employee to volunteer on a regular basis during the day. One teacher recalls with a chuckle a dad who came by every Wednesday on his way to work. One morning he got a call on his cellular phone and the teacher heard him say, "I'll talk to you later about that, I'm reading to the second grade right now."

Schools hold parent-teacher conferences from early in the morning to late at night to accommodate parents, and some hold them on more than one occasion in the semester to provide even more flexibility. Some PTAs hold breakfast meetings, afternoon meetings, and night meetings at various times during the year to provide more of a choice for working parents.

For certain occasions, parents seem to be willing to take off work, such as one school's Manic Monday each year when parents come to school with their children and follow their children's schedules all day.

Single-Parent Family

These are parents whose time and energy are certainly at a premium. They may want to do all they can for their children but need help themselves in coping with the demands placed on them. Flexibility is a must if you hope to see this parent at school.

A Minnesota high school has set up support groups to assist students and to provide increased communication with single parents to keep them informed.

A Kansas high school has trained four counselors on how to meet the needs of single parents and their children. A Texas elementary school uses mentors for most of the boys who have no male role models in the family.

A Washington high school has two counselors and a student assistance team that provide needed support. They offer special programs for students who don't have much money, and joint problem-solving sessions for students and teachers. Some schools send two mailings to parents who are divorced. One high school provides a homework room for students to stay after school.

Blended Family

It is important to keep these families informed and to keep the focus on what is best for each child.

A Washington middle school uses school counselors for outreach and to hold weekly groups that support and assist these students.

Grandparents-as-Parents Family

A high school in the Midwest learned that its faculty and staff needed to constantly remain aware that grandparents in this role are facing an enormous task and that the school must be on guard not to do things that make it more difficult for them. School counselors aware of these problems initiate contact to provide information and to answer any questions that grandparents might have.

One high school in the Northwest assists grandparents acting as parents by offering lots of phone contact and providing regular updates on student responsibilities and graduation requirements.

One elementary school offered training in the "new math" because many grandparents couldn't help their grandchildren with math homework.

Non-English-Speaking Family

Many of these parents are recent immigrants who do not speak or read English and who are unfamiliar with the American public school system. If they are educated, often they need only learn the new language before they are acclimated to their new land and its institutions. But, if they have received little or no education in their native land, they may be completely intimidated by American schools and American educators or they may not share or understand our value of education.

Schools bridge the gap in a number of creative ways. They organize support groups for newly arrived parents, offer ESL classes for adults, record the school's phone message in two or more languages, send out printed material in different languages, and provide translators for meetings and conferences.

A high school on the west coast hires bilingual teachers when possible; has a bilingual student advocate for the counseling office; and has bilingual, bicultural paraprofessionals to work in classrooms. They also contracted with a local counseling agency to assist them in conducting a needs assessment for Hispanic youths and their parents. In addition, they sponsor a Spanish Club, a Cultural Awareness Club, a mariachi music group, and folkloric dancers.

A Minnesota high school holds Asian American parent meetings to encourage involvement from this growing population in the community. The meetings were begun after the school discovered that parents, anxious about not being English proficient, were leaving communication between home and school up to the student. Parents are now attending cocurricular events, calling in absences, and feeling like they have a say in their children's education.

Many mothers in immigrant families do not work and are socially and culturally isolated. Schools that provide social occasions for these women, where they can come together to sew or simply to visit, often find increased family support and involvement because the school is now seen as being a friendly, welcoming place.

Transient Family

One elementary school gives students, on the day they arrive, special guided tours by student ambassadors.

A Washington high school provides a migrant home visitor, a P.A.S.S. study program (Portable Assisted Study Sequence) to help students catch up, and .25 credit options.

Administrators at a Dallas junior high continually work with nearby owners and managers of multifamily complexes, helping devise leasing policies that encourage family stability, such as eliminating the "one month free move-in special." Also of help to transient students is the fact that Texas requires adherence to a consistent statewide core curriculum at all schools.

Because a Kansas high school sponsors a Youth Crisis Shelter facility, they frequently deal with students who are at their school for only a short time. Because these children often require extra time and attention, they are placed in classes with teachers who are identified as best able to work with this type of student.

Same-Sex-Parents Family

A suburban elementary school in the South uses a program that provides a role model of the opposite sex of the parents at home. If the student is identified as at risk, he or she is paired with an adult in the building to visit with daily, one who is willing to provide a support system.

The key is that school staff remain nonjudgmental and open to family involvement, even when a family is nontraditional.

Multicultural Family

A Minnesota high school holds multicultural parent meetings four times a year that are led by a diversity specialist. Discussion focuses on issues of particular interest to multicultural students.

Emancipated Students

A Montana high school has a number of students who live either alone or with neither a parent nor guardian. They present a challenge due to the student's limited legal status. The school works with social agencies, where appropriate, and focuses on building self-esteem and treating all students with respect.

Don't Assume Too Much About Families

We must be careful not to automatically assume anything about our school families other than what we know as fact.

Youngsters from all kinds of families turn out bad, and youngsters from all kinds of families turn out fine. Without knowing the facts of each home situation, it's not wise to assume that because a child is from a certain "type" of family, we know what goes on in that family. If we are to help families succeed in the 1990s, we first have to discard our stereotypes of how certain families function and our preconceptions of their strengths and weaknesses.

All families can help their children succeed. What they do to help the child matters more than whether the family is rich or poor, whether parents finished high school or not, whether they are married or not, whether they have one child or five, or whether their ancestors have been here for generations or arrived yesterday.[8]

Change in education has always exhibited a bit of the "bandwagon" mentality, and it's very much the thing now to lay the blame for all sorts of society's ills on single-parent families. They must take their share of responsibility, as we all must. But to blame one-parent families for all that is being heaped on them today is based more on hysteria than fact and doesn't take into account the many strengths of individual parents. A recent study found that eating meals as a family was associated with a bigger difference in school performance than was having two parents in the home.[9]

There is no denying that single-parent families face serious challenges. After all, it's hard enough for two parents to raise children in a consumer-driven society in which young people are constantly told that the way to be popular and happy is to buy a certain brand of athletic shoes, or cosmetics, or jeans, or soft drinks, or toys. Let's face it, America today is a society in which there is great and growing inequity between the "haves" and "have-nots"; where too many politicians would rather put money into prisons than in early intervention and prevention programs; where members of the music and entertainment industry are more interested in profits than in the influence they have on young minds.

Changing Values

It would not be possible for me to mention the word "family" so often in this book and not talk about "family values." If I didn't, I would be the first writer in the past 5 years not to do so. This also means that I can't forget to bring in a few words about the "African village." And I fully intend to do just that.

We read and hear so much about family values these days. In fact, we can't seem to get away from the subject. (Thanks, Dan Quayle and Murphy Brown!) But as we approach the 21st century, we need to face up to what many of our young people go through every day. Some of the statistics are frightening.

The following happens every day in America:

- 15 children are killed by firearms. (Since 1979, over 50,000 children have been killed by guns.)
- 342 children under 18 are arrested for violent crimes.
- 1,407 babies are born to teen mothers.
- 2,660 babies are born into poverty.
- 2,833 children drop out of school.
- 6,042 children are arrested.
- 8,493 children are reported abused or neglected.
- 100,000 children are homeless.
- 135,000 children take guns to school.[10]

Squabbles between think-tank pundits of both the Right and Left leave us wondering who is to blame for the national chaos and violence in our society.

Politicians use our nostalgia for the "good old days" to make negative comparisons with present-day society. Preachers warn about our loss of virtue. Publishers flood bookshelves with volumes on the decline of morality. Talk show hosts parade before us all kinds of strange people who exemplify dysfunctionality. The nightly news reports on children and families caught in the most tragic of circumstances.

We have to keep reminding ourselves that most children and most families are okay—that most kids from all kinds of families avoid the hazards of dropping out, abusing drugs or alcohol, getting into trouble with the law, and having psychological and emotional problems.

The family is the strength of our society and the passing on of family values is what keeps our nation going, generation after generation. We expect families to teach their children, by both words and actions, the values we have come to recognize as necessary for a quality life in a civilized society—and most families do.

Seven Good Practices for Families

The U.S. Department of Education has recently developed a program called America Goes Back to School: A Place for Families and the Community. This initiative encourages everyone to "go back to school" to share their talents and experiences on an ongoing basis.

Secretary of Education Richard Riley affirms his belief in the importance of helping parents help children. "The American family is the bedrock on which a strong education foundation must be built to prepare our children for the rigors of the 21st century."[11]

Riley's Seven Good Practices for Families

1. Take the time. Those moments talking at evening meals and visiting the library, museum, or zoo make a difference.

2. Read together. It's the starting point of all learning. Read with your youngsters. Share a good book with your teen.

3. Use TV wisely. Limit viewing to no more than 2 hours a school day.

4. Stay in regular contact with your child's teacher. Encourage your child to take challenging courses at school. Check homework every day.

5. Join with your child's teachers and principal to compare your school program against high standards of excellence so your children can reach their full potential.

6. Know where your children are, especially your teens. Encourage them to join youth groups. Support community efforts to keep children safe and off the streets after hours.

7. Talk directly to your children about the values you want them to have and about the dangers of drugs, alcohol, and tobacco—it could literally save their lives.

Notes

1. General Board of Higher Education and Ministry, *Education: The gift of hope.* Nashville, TN: United Methodist Church, 1996.

2. Harold Hodgkinson, *Bringing tomorrow into focus: Demographic insights into the future.* Washington, DC: Institute for Educational Leadership, January 1996.

3. Center on National Education Policy, *Do we still need public schools?* Washington, DC: Author, 1996.

4. Children's Defense Fund, *The state of America's children, yearbook 1996.* Washington, DC: Author, 1996.

5. Stephanie Coontz, "The American family and the nostalgia trap." *Phi Delta Kappan,* March 1995.

6. S. L. Dauber and J. L. Epstein, "Parents' attitudes and practices of involvement in inner-city elementary and middle schools." In N. Chavkin (Ed.), *Families and schools in a pluralistic society.* Albany: State University of New York Press, 1993.

7. Benjamin S. Bloom, *Human characteristics and school learning.* New York: McGraw-Hill, 1976.

8. J. S. Coleman, E. Q. Campbell, C. J. Hobson, J. McPartland, A. M. Mood, F. D. Weinfeld, and R. L. York, *Equality of educational opportunity.* Washington, DC: Government Printing Office, 1996.

9. Coontz, "The American family."

10. Children's Defense Fund, *The state of America's children.*

11. Richard W. Riley, *The family involvement partnership for learning.* U.S. Department of Education. Washington, DC: Government Printing Office, 1996.

Involvement Evaluation

1. List a few things that you particularly liked about the so-called "good old days" that are missing today in education.

_____

_____

_____

_____

Which of these things is it realistically possible to bring back as they were then?

_____

_____

_____

_____

Which are possible to bring back in an altered form? Explain.

_____

_____

_____

_____

2. How has the population of your school changed in the past 10 years?

_____

_____

_____

_____

In the past 5 years?

_____

_____

_____

_____

In the past 2 years?

_____

_____

_____

_____

Acknowledging these trends, do you expect your enrollment to grow, decline, or remain stable over the next 2-3 years?

_____

_____

_____

_____

Do you foresee a major change in the racial or ethnic composition of your students? Explain.

_____

_____

_____

_____

_____

In the economic composition?

_____

_____

_____

_____

_____

3. On the first line, estimate the percentage of students that come from the following types of families. On the second line, after doing further research, does that percentage change or remain the same? (There will be overlapping and your percentages will add up to more than 100%.)

Traditional family   ____ ____

Two-income family   ____ ____

Single-parent family   ____ ____

Blended family   ____ ____

Adoptive family   ____ ____

Grandparents-as-parents family   ____ ____

Non-English-speaking family   ____ ____

Foster family   ____ ____

Transient family   ____ ____

Same-sex-parents family   ____ ____

Combined-household family   ____ ____

Multicultural family   ____ ____

Emancipated students   ____ ____

4. Try to describe the present demographics of your school in three sentences or less.

_____

_____

_____

_____

_____

3 Reaching Out to Parents and Families

Getting and Keeping Them Involved

Why We Join Groups----And Why We Remain Active

If you belong to a professional association, civic group, social club, or charitable organization, think about your participation. Why did you join this particular group? Are you an active member? If so, what does the organization do to sustain your interest? If you are no longer active, ask yourself why. Is it lack of time or lack of motivation? Have your interests changed? Has the organization changed?

We join organizations and associate ourselves with groups for a variety of reasons, but primarily we do so because, as individuals, we derive some benefit from our involvement and association. We may join to advance ourselves professionally, extend our network of contacts, support a cause in which we strongly believe, or simply have a safe, comfortable social outlet. Regardless of our reasons, we select groups that somehow reflect our personal beliefs and value systems.

Parents get involved and stay involved in their child's education and in their child's school for the same reason: There is benefit to be gained. The primary benefit they are seeking is for their child; the secondary benefit is for their child's school. Of course, personal satisfaction must also be factored into the equation.

Groups that successfully involve members in active participation have several attributes:

- The group has a specific purpose or mission.
- Members share a common interest and goals.

- Members have an opportunity to serve in leadership roles.
- Members are encouraged to participate in group projects and activities.
- Leaders communicate clearly with members and solicit their input.
- Members' ideas are respected and their contributions are valued.
- Member participation is recognized, and individual and group achievements are celebrated.
- A spirit of camaraderie prevails.

These same concepts apply to keeping parents active in your school. If you are sincerely committed to parent involvement, you must incorporate these key elements.

Everyone's an Expert on Education

There are few other enterprises—outside of education—where everyone's an expert. Because everybody went to school, everybody has an opinion about what schools should be like and how they should be run.

Because you can't implement every suggestion from parents or please everyone (and wouldn't even if you could), it is important to have a formalized way of involving parents so that their participation in the process of education supports the mission of the school, motivates their children to learn, can be measurably tied to student achievement, and makes them feel valued as a partner and contributor. If you want to get and keep parents on your team, you must provide an opportunity for meaningful, purposeful involvement.

Becoming Purposeful[1]

What is your purpose for involving parents? Exactly how can parents help your school? Exactly how can they help the students?

You will not be able to involve parents unless you provide opportunities and jobs that are purposeful and satisfying. If parents see no purpose for their participation, they will not volunteer; if they see no benefit from their involvement, they will not remain. Parents are busy people and selective in committing their time and efforts.

Following are seven steps to help you form purposeful groups.

Suggested Areas for Purposeful
Family and Community Involvement

1. Identify the specific areas where you want or need parent or family involvement. Suggestions include the following:

Tutoring
Mentoring
Working in the classroom
Library aides
Clerical help
Assisting with special programs
Helping in the office
Helping the school nurse
Assisting with registration
Helping teachers prepare materials (such as laminating, cutting shapes, preparing games)
Decorating bulletin boards
Fundraising
Campus beautification/graffiti patrol
Safety (playground, neighborhood safehouses)
Family activity nights
Student recognition/awards programs
New family orientation
Parenting classes
Family crisis assistance
Before- and after-school programs
Cultural diversity programs
Discipline policy
Curriculum committees
School improvement teams
School site councils
Chaperoning
Booster clubs
Holiday party helpers
Field trips

It is critical that faculty and staff be involved in this first step because they will be the front line of interaction with parents. Faculty and staff must feel comfortable to ensure success. Remember that one of the identified characteristics of successful parent involvement programs is school staff's making it a priority. Include support staff as well as teaching staff.

2. Survey parents to determine their specific areas of interest. Base your survey on the wants and needs identified by faculty and staff, but also allow parents the opportunity to suggest areas you may not have considered. This may bring to light an unknown concern. Survey all parents yearly to determine current areas of interest and concern.

3. Compare your needs and parents interests; develop groups based on areas that match. Parents will help if they work in an area in which they have an interest and feel comfortable. Even though there may be a great need, if volunteers don't like doing certain jobs, they won't continue—and you may lose them for good. Remember, these are volunteers, not employees.

Don't organize too many groups at once. It is important for groups to experience success in their endeavors if they are to remain viable and contributing entities. You are better off to start small, and build your credibility as a school that treats parents as partners—and then add from there.

4. Set parameters, goals, and objectives for each group. If the PTO or PTA or booster club is your fundraising arm, then the school improvement team or site council should not be expected to get involved in those kinds of activities. Clarify your expectations for each group, and make sure that each group understands the role of the other.

Groups need to be able to communicate effectively with each other and support each other's projects. If the school improvement team or site council determines that the school needs money for a specific project, they might want to present that request to the PTA or PTO for assistance.

You want to promote cooperation between the various parent groups. You might even create a special council of representatives from each group that meets on a regular basis to update each other and discuss collaborative efforts to benefit the school.

5. Continuously communicate and recruit. You want to keep your school community updated on the activities being conducted by your parent and community groups. Extend an open invitation for others to join at any time. Groups themselves should do this, of course, but it is important that it also be done through "official" communications as well. Parents are unlikely to become legitimately involved unless they sense a sincere effort by the principal and staff encouraging them to become part of the educational process.

6. Evaluate effectiveness. Ask volunteers to fill out anonymous evaluation instruments on programs in which they have participated, as well as on the overall attitude of school personnel with whom they have worked. You might also have school personnel complete an evaluation as well. Valuable suggestions will come from both groups.

To keep parents involved and to attract new parents, it is important to be able to show in concrete ways how their participation is having an effect on the school and on their children's education. For example, report on how their work on the discipline policy reduced the number of detentions in a semester, show how reading scores went up after implementation of a tutoring program, or relate how attendance increased dramatically when an event was parent sponsored.

7. Celebrate achievements. Remember that parents are volunteers. Thank them regularly during the school year. Thank them personally. Thank them with a note of appreciation. Let them know how much the school depends on them and how much of a difference their participation makes.

Volunteers should also be recognized publicly for the time they devote and the effort they give to the school. Perhaps a way to do this would be with an end-of-the-year tea, banquet, breakfast, celebration, or ceremony at which they are honored and awarded a certificate of appreciation from the school. You might include an article in the newsletter thanking them and listing their names at various times throughout the year.

Strategies for Involvement

In her book *Parents Are Lifesavers,* Carol S. Batey says,

> One way of thinking about parents is to recognize that they are already involved in education. Parenting begins at conception for better or worse. It is a demanding and complex job that is directly related to the self-esteem of the caretakers. When they discover that becoming involved at school makes them feel good about themselves and their families, they want to get even more involved. It is the school's responsibility to help parents embark on this effort.[2]

Batey has identified seven strategies used in successful parent involvement programs for connecting schools and parents.

1. *Extend an invitation.* Create a climate between faculty and parents that lets everyone know parents are needed at school.
2. *Ensure safety.* An orderly atmosphere and a feeling of physical safety within the school building and its surroundings are as important for parents as for children.
3. *Develop a mission.* Shared vision and values, inclusion in the decision-making process, and a focus for working together lead to success.
4. *Empower all parents.* Encouraging parents to be involved in decision and management processes empowers them and raises their self-worth and self-esteem.
6. *Blend diverse interests.* Schools, parents, and students are strengthened by celebrating diversity, multiculturalism, and unity in education.
7. *Communicate with parents.* Clear communication is key to creating a successful parent involvement program.

Parents in Decision-Making Roles

Allowing parents an opportunity to participate in the decision-making process of the school has become one of the key factors in creating a climate that welcomes and values parents.

Authors David C. Berliner and Bruce J. Biddle tell us,

> As a rule, parents are more likely to involve themselves in the school if they feel that they have some degree of control over what goes on in the school and that they can influence their children's education. Thus, schools should not only encourage parental involvement, but they should also set up mechanisms that allow parents to have a say in school policies and procedures. At a minimum, this argues for the creation of school councils and parent-teacher associations; but it may also suggest other mechanisms to promote morale, commitment, and feelings of control among parents.[3]

Don't worry, you won't be inundated with parents who want to run your school. Through their annual survey of parents, a New England school has learned that only a few parents want to be involved directly in issues of school governance. They have found, however, that many want to participate in other areas of the school and in issues related to raising their children.

Barriers to Involvement

Parents themselves have identified some barriers created by the stresses and strains of modern life that prevent them from active involvement in their child's education.

Lack of time. Two thirds of employed parents with children under age 18 say they do not have enough time for their children. (Doesn't that sound like your own life?)

Lack of guidance. Many parents say they would be willing to spend more time on learning activities with their children if teachers would give them direction. Educators also need guidance in working with families because few teacher preparation courses cover the subject.

Lack of community support. Many neighborhoods lack easy access to libraries, cultural institutions, health services, and recreation. This limits home and after-school opportunities for parents to work with their children.

Language and cultural barriers. It's important that we not alienate parents by making assumptions or labeling them as hard to reach or difficult to work with. Instead of looking at them as the problem, we need to look within ourselves at our attitudes and at our methods of communication. Educators need to reach all parents to assure them that the role they play in their child's education is a vital one and that their child's school needs and wants their involvement.

Negative experiences in school. One of the obstacles to overcome with parents is their own personal history related to education. Parents come to us with a lot of baggage. Their own experiences as students strongly affect their attitude toward and interaction with their child's school. If parents remember school in a negative way, they may come to you defensive or even hostile. They may feel intimidated by the school environment and purposely stay away, not because they don't want to help their child, but because it makes them feel ineffective or is a painful reminder of their own past failures.

On the other hand, if their own school experience was positive, they will not only want the same for their child, they will likely want all the extras you can provide as well. These parents feel comfortable in the school environment (sometimes to the degree where they are there so much it begins to interfere with school operations). In both cases, parents are seeking the best possible educational environment for their children based on their own experiences and the role their own parents modeled for them.

Obstacles to Overcome

Too often, we are quick to label certain parents as hard to reach. In the course of our busy schedules, it's easy to make excuses for not taking the time and effort to figure out how to reach them.

A study conducted by Don Davies of the Institute for Responsive Education examined the relationships between hard-to-reach parents and the school. The conclusion reached was that most of the parents in the study were, in fact, reachable but that schools were either not really trying to involve them or were not knowledgeable about or sensitive enough to overcome cultural and social class barriers.

Davies has identified several barriers that limit school involvement for so-called hard-to-reach parents:[4]

- Children from families not conforming to middle-class norms are often seen by school officials as being children who will have trouble in school.
- Communication between schools and poor families is mostly negative. Most of these parents are contacted only when their child is in trouble.
- Teachers and administrators appear to think of these families as being deficient (as families) and concentrate on the problems rather than on the strengths of these families.
- School staff tends to believe that the problems connected with reaching these parents are the fault of parents, not the schools.
- Many poverty-level families have a low assessment of themselves in their ability to be involved in their children's schooling.

Most parents from all groups studied expressed a strong desire to be involved in their children's schooling.

Tips for Involving Parents

One of the pitfalls of labeling families as hard to reach or disinterested is that it causes us to make assumptions about how families function that may in fact apply to very few of them. If we are truly committed to involving families and meeting their needs, we should ask them what those needs and wants are. Often, local people are more effective than outsiders in identifying problems.

Studies continue to show that parents from all walks of life are interested in becoming involved in their children's schooling. It is up to educators to figure out how to reach them and how to make their involvement a positive, productive experience.

1. Be approachable and nonjudgmental (greet at the door, meet outside of office).
2. Reach out, don't wait for them to come to you.
3. Be creative. Try nontraditional approaches (shopping centers, walking neighborhoods, coffees, working with churches).
4. Enlist help from other parents.
5. Be flexible and service oriented (accommodate parents' schedules, offer several choices of days and time, provide child care and transportation).
6. Offer informal workshops (topics on things that make their lives easier, healthier, safer).
7. Respond to calls or contacts in a timely manner (always within 24 hours. If you can't give them an answer within 24 hours, at least let them know that you are working on it and will get back to them when you have something to report—and then get back to them).
8. Follow up participation with appreciation.

Bridging the Communications Gap With Minorities

Public relations specialist Ellen Morgan[5] suggests the following strategies for communicating with minorities:

- Have a diverse representation in your publications and other visuals.
- Build diversity on your staff.
- Have a board policy statement on cultural diversity to set the tone for a school's action plan.
- Involve minorities on advisory committees, boards, and key organizations; be sensitive about leadership roles.
- Keep up to date on the changing school population and its diversity.
- Have Key Communicator groups of ethnic minorities.
- Use community liaisons in your minority Key Communicator groups to reach out to the community.
- If you have a racial incident, ideas on how to resolve the issue may come from your Key Communicator group. (Explain what is being done and enlist their help; perhaps they can mediate.)

- Consider different locations other than the school grounds for meetings when parents or others in the community are involved.
- Provide language translators, if needed, for parents and others in the community.
- Know if parents can read in their own language.
- Work with the minority media and the mainstream media's special feature sections.

Reaching Goals

Think about your *personal goals*. Think about the *goals you have for your school*. Think about the *goals you have for the students*.

List those goals under the three headings just mentioned.

Do you need help in achieving these goals—or can you do it all alone? Silly question, of course you can't. You need help from your faculty, from your staff, from the district, and from the taxpayers.

Can you use additional help? Well, unless your school is located in an extremely wealthy district whose taxpayers are begging to give your district all the money it needs and your school all the money you ask for, the answer is a resounding "Yes!"

And from where is this help to come? I can think of two accessible places, one is from business partnerships and the other is from (you guessed it!) *volunteers*!

They're out there, you need 'em, now go get 'em!

Notes

1. Karen H. Kleinz, Kleinz Communications, Peoria, Arizona, National School Public Relations Association southwest vice president. Training material.

2. Carol S. Batey, *Parents are lifesavers: A handbook for parent involvement in schools.* Thousand Oaks, CA: Corwin, 1996.

3. David C. Berliner and Bruce J. Biddle, *The manufactured crisis, myths, fraud, and the attack on America's public schools.* Reading, MA: Addison-Wesley, 1995.

4. Don Davies, "Benefits of and barriers to parent involvement." *Community Education Research Digest*, 2(2), 1988.

5. Ellen T. Morgan, The Morgan Group, Tujunga, California, former National School Public Relations Association vice president at large for minority relations. Training material.

Involvement Evaluation

1. Think of an organization with which you are presently involved, or in which you have been involved in the past. List three to

five things about the group that you particularly liked, things that kept you interested and involved.

_____

_____

_____

_____

List three to five things you liked least, things that may have contributed to your no longer being involved.

_____

_____

_____

_____

How can you relate these characteristics to how your volunteers might feel about their involvement at your school?

_____

_____

_____

2. What is your purpose or goal for involving parents in your school?

_____

_____

_____

Is that goal realistic? How long will it take to accomplish?

_____

_____

_____

What will you personally have to do to accomplish it?

_____

_____

_____

3. List three ways that parents can help your school this year. Be specific.

_____

_____

_____

List three ways they can help students.

_____

_____

_____

4. What do you see as the function of your PTA/PTO/Booster Club/parent groups? Do these organizations see their function in the same way as you see it?

_____

_____

_____

_____

5. List the 10 people by name that you would most like to see become involved or more involved with your school. What could you do to involve each one?

_____

_____

_____

_____

6. How often do you communicate with parents? What methods do you use for communication?

_____

_____

_____

_____

7. Do you evaluate the effects of parent participation programs? How?

_____

_____

_____

8. How do you thank parents, and how often?

_____

_____

_____

9. What decision-making roles are parents allowed?

_____

_____

_____

10. What do you perceive as the three main barriers to parental involvement in your school?

_____

_____

_____

Which of these barriers is it possible to overcome?

_____

11. Have you specifically tried to recruit minorities?

_____

_____

_____

How have you bridged the communication gap?

_____

_____

_____

4 Parent and Family Involvement Programs That Work

The Best Ideas From the Best Schools

Benefits of Involvement

Our students benefit from involvement because their family members are more aware of programs and scholarship opportunities. Parents have a clearer understanding of the school's expectations for students. Through the year we provide information to parents through phone contacts, newsletters, referrals, and letters of commendation. When students have a successful educational experience, postsecondary educational opportunities are enhanced and students have a better future. Families benefit through resources made available to them. [We have] a great school because our parents and community members help us to support all of our students in their curricular and extracurricular programs. (Principal Joan Wright, Wenatchee High School, Washington)

Family involvement at our school has resulted in increased attendance to over 92% per month and improved behavior in students with discipline problems. (Principal Perry Sandler, Joseph Pulitzer Middle School, Jackson Heights, New York)

We are committed to promoting student learning through parent partnerships that involve parents in their child's education; that foster shared responsibility among students, parents, and staff; and that link families with school and community resources. We encourage broad-based representation in the decision-making process because we believe parents make a difference. (Principal Susan Van Zant, Morning Creek Elementary School, San Diego, California)

Parent involvement impacts our school in every area. Volunteers serve lunch; act as workroom aides, library aides, office aides, and classroom aides; coordinate bulletin board and showcase usage; present unit studies; work with small groups of children; assist in computer labs and with special programs and productions; and help plan and drive for field trips—among other things.

Parents who work full time are often involved by working on projects at home. A Volunteer Coordinator aids in placement of volunteers to optimize volunteer effectiveness. The motivation behind the high level of parental activity in our school is the voiced appreciation and gratefulness openly expressed by the staff. Volunteerism permits a greater scope of learning opportunities to exist, such as field trips, cooking, art projects, etc. Parental experience and talent is showcased in the classroom for special unit studies such as Alaskan careers, foreign languages, ethnic cuisine, animal caretaking, music, arts, and drama. Parents return this appreciation of their efforts with a respect for the authority of the classroom educator and a respect for school district policies and procedures. This mutual recognition and appreciation promotes an atmosphere of teamwork and partnership in education. (Principal Donna Peterson, North Star Elementary Schools, Nikiski, Alaska)

How Parents Can Make a Difference

Strong Families, Strong Schools,[1] a research-based report on family involvement from the U.S. Department of Education, includes a list of steps parents can take to connect with their child and with their child's school.

At home, parents can do the following:

- Read with their children and together as a family.
- Use TV wisely.
- Establish a daily family routine.
- Schedule daily homework times.
- Monitor out-of-school activities.
- Talk with children and teenagers.
- Communicate positive values and character traits, such as respect, hard work, and responsibility.
- Express high expectations and offer praise and encouragement for achievement.

At their child's school, parents can do the following:

- Ensure that middle and secondary students are offered and enrolled in challenging courses.
- Keep in touch with the school instead of waiting until a problem arises.
- Ask more from schools, such as higher learning standards, better discipline, safer environment, mentoring and tutoring programs, career counseling, internships in vocational and technical studies, and increased family involvement.
- Use community resources, such as after school and summer programs, library and cultural services, adult education classes, recreation facilities.

- Encourage employers to be school and family friendly by building partnerships with schools, adopting policies that allow parents to spend time in their child's school, donating expertise or money or supplies, providing mentors, and sponsoring school-to-work programs.

At-Home Involvement Strategies

The involvement strategies described in this chapter are included because these programs have been effective at one or more schools. The ideas come from principals, teachers, and parents and from elementary, middle, and high schools all across the country.

PTA Newsletter

At a Dallas junior high, one of their most successful communication tools is the PTA newsletter. Published six times a year, it contains letters and articles from administrators and counselors and information about upcoming activities, describes club and organization activities, and announces awards and accomplishments. The first issue is mailed 2 weeks prior to the start of school and details registration procedures and get-acquainted activities for new students. Parents also publish a directory of all students and, most important, their phone numbers.

Principal's Newsletter

A Wisconsin high school with a student population of 400 publishes a monthly newsletter from the principal. Included is a summary of the Parent Advisory Council meetings, the next month's calendar of events, parenting ideas, and a short paragraph about each grade's "student of the month." The newsletter includes a "Happy Birthday" column where the names of all students who have a birthday that next month are listed according to birth dates. In May, the birthdays for June, July, and August are listed. There are a lot of computer-generated graphics in this newsletter; almost every article has at least one picture or illustration.

Newsletter With Academic Information

A small inner-city middle school in the Midwest sends out a monthly four-to-six-page newsletter. The first page consists of a letter from the principal, usually about adolescent behavior and offering hints on how parents can help young teens.

On the other pages, each teacher in the school writes a paragraph. This paragraph includes what the class will be covering that month, what the student is expected to learn, specific assignments, and dates of upcoming tests. For example, the social studies instructor might write that the class will be studying the Civil War, its causes, main battles, and effects on civilians; that a book report on someone connected with the Civil War is due on such and such a date; a listing of several major homework assignments; and test dates for the upcoming month. Teachers keep their paragraph(s) concise but include enough detail so that parents will know what their children are expected to do that month.

Reading-at-Home Program

A Michigan elementary district has a program, sponsored by a local business, that gives prizes for reading one book a week at home. The parent signs a card that the book was read and that a brief synopsis of the story was told to them. Prizes include pizza coupons, radios, money banks, books, T-shirts, Frisbees, and so on.

Assignment Book for Parents to Initial

At an inner-city Indiana middle school that has improved performance greatly, each student is given a book in which he or she writes all homework assignments. The teacher checks to see that the assignment has been entered as the student leaves the classroom. A parent must initial the assignment page each night when homework is completed. If there is no homework, that is indicated as well, and the parent initials as usual.

Weekly Classroom Information for Parents

At the end of each week, teachers at a California elementary school inform parents about what the class as a whole (not individual students) did in school that week. Each day, the teacher briefly records one or two class highlights on preprinted notepaper. These daily summaries accumulate until, on Friday, there are five and the page is full. The note to parents is then duplicated for all class members and sent home with each child. At the bottom of the page, there is space for other information that the teacher might want to include, such as a reminder of an upcoming field trip or a holiday party or a book report due date.

Each teacher has a name for his or her weekly report, such as "Carlson's Chronicles," "Pearson's Press," or "Ingram's Info."

Journal for Students and Parents

A Colorado elementary school, beginning with first grade, has each student write weekly in a notebook journal. The child takes it home each week so parents can also write in it. This fosters communication between parents and child, allows parents to see their child's writing progress, and is a keepsake when the book is taken home at the end of the year.

Borrowing Computers for Home Use

An inner-city Phoenix elementary district has computers that can be checked out and taken home temporarily or for the whole school year. To qualify, both parent and student must attend a training session. Each teacher is asked to recommend families for this program.

Interactive Homework

A sixth-grade teacher in Iowa has several assignments during the year requiring children to interview family members or friends, for example, a report on personal experiences of the Depression Years or of World War II, a family history, a memorable Christmas, or a contact with a famous person.

Three-Week Grade Report

An Arizona high school sends a grade report home every 3 weeks. Initially, teachers were not enthusiastic because of the extra work involved. But after a few months, complaints ceased due to several factors.

First, preparing these triweekly reports was not as time consuming as expected. Because all teachers are required to keep their grades on computer anyway, each grade notice is printed out, then given to the student to take home. No signature is required from parents, but parents are informed several times during the year (in the handbook, by newsletter, at Open House, etc.) to look for these grade notices.

Second, parents find out when their son or daughter first begins to fall behind. They know to monitor the student's homework, or to call the teacher to discuss where the problem lies—before the student is failing.

Third, parents no longer can use the excuse at the end of the year that no one informed them that their child was failing.

Not a Field Trip

"This is *not* a class field trip. I told the class that I was going whale watching and would tell them when I plan to go. It is a fun family outing, but not inexpensive!"

These were the first three lines of a letter sent by a San Diego elementary school teacher to the parents of her students. The letter went on to give pertinent information about the whale watching excursion, along with an invitation to families to make reservations if they were interested in joining her. Those who wished to go met her on the boat. The teacher was merely offering students and their families an opportunity to see whales, and she took no other responsibility for the trip other than sending the invitation letter. The last line of the letter read, "I will *not* be going if there is a slight chance of stormy weather!"

Phone Calls and Postcards

At a Missouri middle school, teachers are required to make five positive phones calls each week telling a parent about specific academic progress that the child has made. For example, "Mrs. Smith, I just wanted to tell you that Susie made an A on her math test last week. This was her first A and I'm very proud of her. She has been working hard to understand fractions. She listens in class and asks for help when she needs more explanation. And she has been doing all of her homework assignments as well. Thought you would want to know how hard she is trying and how well she is doing."

Teachers also send out postcards each week to five parents with the words "Good News from A. B. Green School" printed at the top. These short messages praise their child's behavior, good manners, extra effort, excellent grades, attendance, outstanding work, special report, or whatever has been particularly noteworthy of late. An example is, "Ms. Roberts: Just a note to let you know that Bill was selected to be a lunchroom monitor for April. This is quite an honor, and I'm very proud of him."

The names of pupils whose parents will be receiving these phone calls and postcards are given to the principal at the beginning of the week. This is to prevent duplications and assures that the same parent isn't contacted by the math, science, and English teachers during the same week.

Student Pride Award

A New Mexico middle school gives a Pride Award for students who don't normally receive recognition. Parents are sent a postcard informing them of this honor.

Videos for Parents

A Southern California elementary school, in cooperation with the county and a local health system, makes videotapes available for parents to watch at home. This program began as an effort to inform parents about the signs and dangers of substance abuse. The results were so positive that the Video Check-Out Program expanded to include other subjects important to parenting. Some of the videos are geared to adults, some to the entire family, others to certain ages. Among the topics available for viewing are alcohol, peer pressure, stepfamilies, dental care, homework, nutrition, smoking, safety, respect, maturation, and self-esteem.

In-School Involvement Strategies

Multiple Notices and Solicitations

A Minnesota middle school sends volunteer sign-up forms out many times during the year instead of just once. They have found that when they keep asking, parents will come forward.

Student Programs at PTA Meetings

A Texas elementary school ensures high attendance at PTA meetings by having a different grade level put on a program at each meeting. The music and art departments are also included at each meeting. The business meeting is never more than 15 or 20 minutes long, and then the grade-level program begins. Every child in the participating grade has some part in the program.

Open Door Policy

An Alaska elementary school has an open door policy that encourages parents to visit the school at any time. The only requirement is an appropriate security check-in at the front office.

School Tours

Once a week, a Minnesota high school invites any parent who wishes to visit the school during the day to come by. The parents are given a tour by the principal and then sent off to see what goes on during a typical school day. Afterward, parents regroup with the principal for a discussion about what they saw and to ask questions.

Principal's Coffee

An Illinois high school principal holds a monthly Principal's Coffee both during the day and in the evening with an open invitation to parents. This informal gathering allows parents to get to know the principal, to communicate their concerns, and to tour the school. Eighth-grade parents have been particularly receptive as they prepare their adolescents for the transition to high school.

Cafecitos

An Arizona elementary school principal holds off-campus cafe meetings (*cafecitos*) with parents to discuss school and education issues.

Parent Organizations

An Arizona high school involves parents through several groups such as the Parent Action Club, Parents Supporting Parents, and the Parent Booster Club. Parents meet in groups to discuss what works and what doesn't in raising teenagers. They also work together to discourage their children from taking drugs or being involved in gangs. One group does fundraising for special needs.

Teacher Wish Lists

The Parent/Teacher/Student Association (PTSA) at an Illinois high school has raised tens of thousands of dollars over the past 5 years to support the purchase of school equipment identified by teachers on their "wish list." PTSA purchases mostly high-tech equipment with this money so that a maximum number of students can benefit. These purchases were especially timely during some recent budget cuts.

Booster Clubs

Most high school have the traditional Booster Clubs where parents help with fundraising and organizational tasks for sports and band. An Illinois high school's Booster Club runs concession stands; sells T-shirts, sweatshirts, and logo items; sponsors "rooter" buses for away games; and offers incentives such as prizes and athletic contests to encourage student attendance.

A Minnesota high school Booster Club took on the task of completing the football stadium by adding a new ticket booth and new bleachers with parents doing much of the work themselves. Their Choir Booster Club was crucial in helping the choir earn funds for a trip to Europe.

Many schools have expanded their traditional athletic Booster Clubs to include other extracurricular activities such as drama, debate, cheerleading, softball, and orchestra.

Major Projects

A few years ago, parents from the Fine Arts Program spearheaded a drive to renovate an Illinois high school's Little Theater. The curtains and the lighting and audio systems were replaced with state-of-the-art computerized equipment. The stage was redone, seats were upholstered, and three backstage areas were built for scenery construction and makeup. This year a group of parents is organizing a fundraising drive to purchase equipment for a new weight training facility.

Supply Room Volunteers

At a Dallas middle school, volunteers stock and maintain the Supply Room and sell school supplies to students every morning before classes begin. They also furnish physical education uniforms for sale at the beginning of the year.

Science Volunteers

An Oregon elementary school has a program in which parents who have a job, hobby, or interest related to science are invited to share their knowledge and love of science with students. The adults make a short presentation (with a demonstration, if possible) and often bring along models, samples, illustrations, specimens, or displays to help explain their subject. Among the fields of expertise covered have been bird-watching, engines, the weather, rocks, oceanography, food processing, gems and jewelry making, and animal psychology.

Music and Drama Volunteers

Each year, a Washington high school puts on a major production, produced in alternate years by the music and drama departments. For the musical *My Fair Lady*, there was a core of 25 adult volunteers who helped with advertising, ticket sales, costumes, set design and building, makeup supervision, dance instruction, and other support functions. Teachers credit the excellent quality of the production to students' hard work and the support that parents and community members provided.

Wanted: Piano Players

A Nevada elementary school advertised in their newsletter seeking someone to play the piano for primary class activities and school programs. Two grandparents came forward and are now actively involved in the music program of the school.

Talent Show

At a Dallas middle school, parents organize, rehearse, and present the annual Talent Show. Volunteers also help during special school events such as pep rallies, assemblies, and picture day.

Chaperones and Security

At an Ohio inner-city high school, parents are always on the scene, and highly visible, as chaperones for dances and for security at sporting events. The school found that fathers wearing special jackets were more effective than either teachers or hired security guards at maintaining order during football games. In fact, before the fathers became involved, the school was seriously considering eliminating interscholastic football.

Fathers from an Indiana school district have formed Security Dads for dances, skating parties, sports contests, and other student-based extracurricular activities. The presence of these dads promotes a safe, drug-free environment.

Classes for Parents

An Ohio school supports families by offering evening parenting and leadership classes, GED classes, child guidance, and family math and science activities. Child care is provided.

Workshops for Parents of Teens

A Minnesota high school sponsors Saturday workshops for parents on adolescent development, parent-teen relationships, preparation for college, conflict management, and time management.

School Advisory Board

A Nebraska high school has a 30-member advisory board with representatives from parents, teachers, students, and the community. They hold at least four monthly breakfast meetings with the principal to discuss ideas, concerns, and plans for school improvement.

A Wisconsin high school holds its Parent Advisory Council monthly meetings in local restaurants.

Lunchtime Programs

At a Kentucky elementary school, programs are held at regular intervals on the cafeteria stage during lunch. This prevents loss of classroom time for events such as a performance by a middle-school choir, a demonstration by high school cheerleaders, a piano recital by a student, or the parent group explaining its candy sale.

Invite Parents for Lunch

A Michigan school has extended parents (and community members) an open invitation to each lunch in the cafeteria. Parents pay for their meal and are only asked to call the office ahead of time so the cafeteria staff will know they're coming.

Bean Bag Buddies

A Texas elementary school has Bean Bag Buddies in which a volunteer and child read together, sitting in a bean bag (if they wish) for half an hour. The volunteer comes on a regular basis and reads with the same child all year. This is great for at-risk kids. Grandparents and senior citizens particularly enjoy this activity.

An Illinois principal listens to each Pre-K–3 student read a book or portion of a book to her. The child and parents are very proud when this happens.

Family Banquet

A Massachusetts high school holds an annual Family Night where all 250 students are celebrated individually. This has evolved from potlucks to a sit-down dinner at the Museum of Science, now one of the school's partners.

FUN—Family Unity Night

Once a month, students at a Missouri middle school bring their parent(s) to school for FUN. Students are not allowed to attend without an adult. Each month, a different activity is planned. Some themes from this past year were fried chicken night, bingo, basketball, ice cream social, pizza party, softball, and board game night. Some activities draw large numbers; others, a small attendance. Refreshments are always available.

At one of the monthly PTA-sponsored family nights at a California elementary school, there is an opportunity to have family or individual portraits taken. Others offerings have been burgers at a nominal price and entertainment by a professional mime.

Family Carnival

An Alaska elementary school holds a winter carnival-type event sponsored by the PTA. It is specifically designed to bring together families from different backgrounds and income levels for the simple purpose of community spirit and a sense of connection.

Family Picnic

A California elementary school holds an annual family picnic. Their local business adopter provides a band and beverages. Families bring their picnic basket and blankets or chairs.

Out-of-Town Trips

A suburban, lower-income Missouri middle school sponsors annual trips to Washington, D.C. and Boston on alternate years. Most students have traveled very little and are eager to raise money for the trip. Parents are required to help at one or more of the fundraisers. Car washes, candy sales, pizza parties, and gift wrap sales are some of the fundraising activities. "When the kids return home and the parents' go to the airport to pick them up, the joy and pride in the parents eyes is something to see." They used to make the trip by bus, but because of the time and hassle involved, they decided to earn a little more and go by plane. Sometimes parents pay their own way and go along.

Buy a Brick

A Texas elementary school built a brick sidewalk in front of the school for the purpose of selling individually engraved bricks as a fundraiser. When several bricks are sold, the plain bricks already in the walk are pried out and the engraved ones put in. There are 6,000 bricks in the walk, so this fundraiser will be ongoing for several years. A brick costs $100, and each year about 50 are sold. Here are some engravings: "Step here for luck"; "The Smith Family 1996"; "Mary Jones, 2nd grade"; "Class of 1995"; "Mr. Green's 4th grade, 1992"; "Go Tigers"; "Thanks, Mrs. Butler, [signed] Mark." All money from this activity goes to buy additional computers or other high-tech equipment for student use.

Gift Wrapping Activity

At the Christmas season, some stores will allow volunteers to staff their gift wrapping department on a part-time or full-time basis (and kids love to help their parents with this activity). All wages go to the school rather than to the individuals. Volunteers must be dependable and somewhat speedy and talented in the skill of gift wrapping, and there always needs to be someone from the group in charge. If a sign is posted at the gift wrap counter saying, "Happy Valley High (or Middle) School students, parents, and teachers are wrapping gifts this Christmas at Sears to earn money for their library," you would be amazed at how patient and friendly customers can be (and sometimes you get donations). No doubt it's the Christmas spirit that mellows all those people waiting in line—as long as the wait is not too long. If this activity is well organized and works out well, the store will come back to you year after year. Teachers and parents and students working together is a great bonding experience—and it's not a "make-work" thing, it's a "real-work" thing.

Back-to-School Parade

An elementary school in a Dallas suburb has a parade just before school begins. Children make banners and placards to carry; the school cooks march, banging their pots and pans; refreshments are sold; members of the community ride in antique cars; lots of neighborhood children join in, including parents with babies in strollers; and school supplies are sold by the PTA. At the end of the parade, the classrooms are opened for an hour so students can find their room and put away their school supplies. Postcards with parade details are sent to all students a few weeks in advance of the fall opening of school.

Thanking Volunteers

A San Diego elementary school tries to let volunteers know throughout the year just how much they are appreciated. They provide coffee during the day, provide food for volunteers at work sessions (Dittoing for Donuts) and special events, send notes of appreciation, and hold a gala Room Parent Tea in June that is hosted by the teachers and attended by over 250 people.

School Buses for Parents

In several districts, parents without transportation are encouraged to make use of the district school bus system. This provides parents with a ride to and from school, and bus drivers with a bus monitor.

A Personal Invitation

A Washington middle school actively recruits parents whenever they visit the school campus. The administrators, faculty, and staff go out of their way to make it known how proud they are of the school's parent involvement. Volunteers are honored in the spring with a formal ceremony.

Junior High Jitters

A Dallas middle school takes great care to ease the transition from elementary school to junior high and from junior high to high school. Parents of sixth graders are welcome to visit classrooms on any day, and Junior High Jitters is a program to answer the questions of parents of incoming seventh graders. Ninth graders and their parents are invited to several spring seminars in preparation for the high school experience.

New Parent Breakfast

A Tennessee school holds a new parent breakfast each year. They also have a family picnic, a health fair, an end-of-the-year reception, and a Parent Appreciation Tea. Parents are also kept informed through newsletters as to the difference their volunteer time makes to the instructional program and the school.

Coffee and Pastry for Newcomers

Several times a year, a Texas elementary school in a fast-growing suburban area holds a morning (7:30 a.m.) coffee and pastry breakfast for newcomers and their children. The parent group provides the pastries. The children go on to their classes at 8:00 and the parents usually remain for a while to get better acquainted.

Family Learning Evenings

A California elementary school offers family evenings focusing on a variety of curricular areas. Parents and students gather to solve problems and learn to work together as they participate in learning experiences. This also allows parents to become knowledgeable about learning styles, assessment procedures, and how they can provide a home environment that contributes to their child's success in school. One event is a Math-Science Night where families work together to solve problems in those subjects.

Parents are invited annually to attend parenting sessions that address issues identified through a survey. They share concerns and discuss child rearing in a comfortable atmosphere.

Full-Time Volunteer Coordinator

A San Diego elementary school has a paid, full-time volunteer coordinator. It is her job to locate and recruit parents and other members of the community to help in the classroom on a regular basis, tutor individual students, serve as group leaders on field trips, and work on specific events such as book fairs, assemblies, and special class projects. Every Tuesday and Thursday, there is a dedicated group of volunteers who assists with preparing classroom materials. Last year, from a student population of 886, 375 volunteers logged over 5,250 hours to provide support to instructional activities.

English/Spanish Meetings

A Washington high school hosts special meetings in English and Spanish for Latino students and their parents. The goal for these meetings is to provide the opportunity for students and parents to voice their needs concerning the educational system, cultural transition, after-school activities, and family and community involvement.

International Teas

An elementary school in Southern California hosts several International Teas during the year. These events provide an opportunity for staff and parents to interact in a relaxed manner and to learn about the school and each other. Community members share their cultural heritage with individual classes and prepare displays for the library.

Classes for Mothers of Immigrant Children

An Arizona inner-city elementary district offers parenting, sewing, and ESL classes to the mothers of immigrant students. The primary goals are to break the pattern of isolation of these women and help them feel a part of their child's school community.

Freshman Orientation Picnic

A Montana high school holds a freshman orientation picnic for incoming ninth graders and their parents.

Yearly Survey

A Kansas high school conducts a yearly survey of students, parents, and staff to determine perceptions about the school. For the survey, 150 students, 100 parents, and 50 staff are chosen at random.

Campus Beautification

A Texas middle school PTSA along with the administration and staff have jointly undertaken to beautify and revitalize their campus. The PTSA has allocated $1,000 for an outdoor study area with tables, benches, and shade trees (which students have helped to plant). The benches and tables provide a shady, peaceful place to relax or study.

Landscaping

The parent group at an Illinois high school spearheaded an aggressive campaign to landscape the school campus. They hired a landscape architect to design a master plan, conducted a fundraising campaign, and entered into a partnership with the city to help plant trees and grass.

Buy a Bush

At a Missouri elementary school, people were offered the opportunity to "buy a bush" for the campus. Over $5,000 was collected, and parents turned out on several Saturdays to help with the planting.

Parent Garden Club

An Allen, Texas elementary school has a Parent Garden Club. A group of fathers has especially enjoyed the trimming and pruning of trees and bushes on campus.

Toddler Room

At an Alaska elementary school, parents with preschoolers are able to volunteer while leaving their small children in a cooperative Toddler Room staffed by volunteers.

Internet Instruction

An Illinois high school invites parents who are interested in getting on-line to an evening of instruction and hands-on experience. Both computer novices and sophisticated users interested in how computers are used in a public school setting are welcome.

Raising Money for Computers

At an Orlando Pre-K–5 school, the parent group has targeted computers and computer equipment as the emphasis for fundraisers. More parents are participating because they are strongly in favor of this goal.

Father-Daughter and Mother-Son Activities

At a K–5 California school, the PTA sponsors a Father-Daughter Valentine Dance for fifth graders; mothers help decorate and bake cookies for the event. For the fifth-grade boys, there is a Mother-Son "Boys' Night Out." Last year, the mothers and sons were entertained with an exciting bicycle launch ramp and trick-riding show. If fathers or mothers can't attend, the student is invited to bring a relative or adult friend.

Club Night

A Dallas middle school PTA hosts an evening to inform students of extracurricular opportunities. The school publishes a booklet with information about school activities and organizations. At Club Night, students visit with club sponsors and select the organization(s) to which they wish to belong. Information is shared with parents, and parents are urged to encourage their child's participation. Most clubs and activities are sponsored by parent volunteers. Parents also help coach group activities such as Academic Pentathlon, Odyssey of the Mind, Texas Youth in Government, and the Debate Team.

Fully 80% of all students at this school belong to at least one organization, and more than 35% of students participate on athletic teams.

Extended Student Services

A California elementary school offers a parent-paid program that provides before- and after-school child care. The program operates during vacations and on nonschool days as well. Parents aren't expected to volunteer in this program, but it has the support of a great many parents who appreciate having a place where their children are able to do homework in a supervised setting, have access to the computer lab, and enjoy a wide variety of learning activities and games. Healthy snacks are provided. These services begin at 6:15 a.m. and continues until 6:00 p.m. Students may also participate in inexpensive after school enrichment courses. These 8-week sessions are offered in dance, athletics, science, computers, hobbies, art, crafts, chorus, foreign languages, and so on. During the school year, about 30% of students participate.

Notice by Mail

A West Virginia middle school recognizes that middle school students are not overjoyed to have their parents involved at school and often are poor school-to-home communicators. Therefore, the school mails newsletters monthly and notifies parents when and where their child is involved in a special activity.

"Real Men Read, Too"

A Texas elementary school started a "Real Men Read, Too" program where dads come and read a story in their child's classroom at least once a year. The dads get their names printed on paint stir sticks, which are tacked onto the library wall.

A Michigan elementary school invites well-known people from the local community, the state, and the nation to be guest readers in their classrooms.

Parent/Teacher Dance

An Illinois high school parent/teacher/student group sponsored a 1950s-style Sock Hop in the gym for adults, not only to raise funds but also to have a fun social event. Everyone dressed in '50s-style clothing; a few even unpacked their letter jackets and sweaters. Students helped with arrangements as well as food sales at the dance. Parents commented that the students were envious because the parents were having so much fun.

An elementary school in South Carolina held a Disco Night for parents and teachers, complete with platform shoes, bell bottoms, and Bee Gees music.

Parent/Teacher/Student Conferences

An Orlando, Florida elementary school uses portfolio assessments at parent/teacher/student conferences at the end of each 12-week period. Goals are set at the conference so that parents can have input. When new students register, parents are told about the assessment process and that their involvement is expected. After 3 years, parent participation at the conferences is at 97%.

For the past 3 years at conferences, an Alaska elementary school has included not only teachers and parents but students as well. It's not uncommon for a student to lead the conference.

Parent/Counselor Conferences

A Washington high school's counseling staff has made school-to-work and career counseling a major goal. In the fall, counselors conduct individual 30-minute conferences with each of the seniors and their parents to discuss post-high-school planning. In the spring, they meet individually with incoming freshman students and their parents to develop a 4-year plan of classes.

The counseling staff hosts evening parent information meetings, which cover a range of topics including standardized test results, financial aid, and Career Center orientation.

Parent/Teacher Conferences

A North Carolina high school has increased its parent/teacher conferences to four a year, allowing them to keep parents better informed of student progress.

A Texas elementary school has had great conference success by encouraging teachers to share their expertise with parents.

Discipline Assistance Program

An Illinois high school has devised a discipline policy that requires parent involvement. The Family Assistance Program (FAP) consists of six sessions that the student and parents must attend in lieu of a 10-day suspension.

First Impressions Are Important

As the saying goes, "You only have one chance to make a good first impression." High schools have a wonderful opportunity to reach parents of eighth-grade students who are excited about their upcoming high school experience—and their parents are often equally enthusiastic. After all, it's not very realistic to expect parents of juniors or seniors to suddenly become involved in school when they haven't shown any previous inclination. But parents of eighth and ninth graders are open to all kinds of possibilities. Sometimes these parents really want to be involved but feel they shouldn't be too visible around their teenagers so they "hang back." If a high school can develop broad, active parent participation, then individual parents are more comfortable and feel it's okay for them to be seen at school because students are so used to seeing parents around school that it's "acceptable."

Sussex Technical High School in Georgetown, Delaware attributes its success with parental involvement to three major initiatives: admissions, communication, and involvement.

Admissions. Eighth graders and their parents receive a mailing of the Program of Studies brochure describing the 16 career options available. Students who elect to enroll attend a Career Day presentation, which is reinforced by a Saturday Open House for parents where they rotate through presentations from each technical area teacher.

Communication. A course schedule is mailed to all students prior to the first day of school, and a day and evening Open House is held so parents and students can visit the school and walk the student's schedule. On Back-to-School Night, parents attend a 3-hour program interacting with their children's teachers. In addition, the school offers newsletters, award programs, conferences, planning and assessment meetings, and a variety of other options for parents.

Involvement. Advisory committees allow parents to lend their expertise to technical programs grouped in four clusters: automotive, business, health and human services, and industrial engineering. Parents in professions related to the majors offered at Sussex serve as guest speakers to discuss job opportunities and careers. So that they can observe their child's mastery of skills, parents are invited to attend the formal research project presentations required of all seniors.

Parent Training Sessions

Travis Middle School in McAllen, Texas has a training program for parents that is intended to empower uneducated or poor parents in methods of making the educational system work for them. They attend classes explaining scheduling, detracking, inclusion, positive conferencing skills, and effective school-to-home and home-to-school communications. These parents also commit to attend one meeting per month with their child's team of teachers and to practice their newly acquired conferencing skills.

The number of irate and disgruntled parents who have taken their complaints to the principal has decreased significantly since last year. Most concerns are now being resolved at the lowest level, and as indicated by a survey of their attitudes toward the school, the majority of parents are very happy with the school's programs.

The number of parents who participate in these weekly parent training sessions has increased dramatically. Whenever the school has an item on the school board agenda, at least 10 to 15 parents attend. In Padre a Padre sessions, the attendance has gone up from an average of 7 parents last year to 25 parents this year. PTSA membership had increased from 120 parents to 250 and those who attend PTSA meetings fill the cafeteria. The first parent training session had an attendance of 80 parents as compared to 12 the previous year. These numbers are exceptional for an inner-city middle school.

Parents have organized a Campus Improvement Plan. The Leadership Council continuously works on discipline and curriculum changes. A Parent Task Force came about as part of a plan developed during one of the training sessions. This task force provides supervision for students during the day in the halls, and in the cafeteria and courtyard during lunch hours. The presence of the task force helps provide a safe, protective environment. Members of the task force wear special vests for identification. Through their efforts, a crossing guard has been hired and parents have volunteered to direct traffic after school. They also visit parents in their homes to discuss the link between student behavior and achievement.

The key to the success of this school's active parental involvement lies in the quality of the personnel involved and their dedication to the program. Bimonthly training sessions are held for the core group of parent leaders, as well as for others who are interested. Grant funding has helped provide stipends to cover the costs of baby-sitting, travel, and meals. The program has proved to be a good investment for the school as well as for the low-income parents. Without such stipends, getting those parents to come to school on a regular basis is difficult. It also eliminates the trouble of trying to accommodate small children and babies during training sessions.

Dealing With Controversial Issues

At a Missouri middle school in a suburban, upper-income, conservative neighborhood, the principal organized an Advisory Committee composed of 12 members (4 parents from each grade) who met once a month at 7:00 in the evening (a beverage and dessert were always served). The committee had a staggered rotation every 3 months.

Whenever a controversial issue arose, the principal brought it up for discussion before the Advisory Committee. For example, should an AIDS prevention film be shown, and if so, should it be shown to sixth graders? Interest in issues was always high at advisory meetings, and often discussions continued in the parking lot after adjournment.

If parents had a concern or had heard a rumor, they were expected to bring it up to the principal and the committee. These were not meetings for just talking and getting acquainted—the principal always had an agenda. Often, the principal was able to get a sense of what direction to take or how to solve a problem just by listening to the parents talk.

Parent participation was high because their commitment was appreciated, their opinions valued, and their influence strong. Yet their time commitment was short—only three meetings in 3 months. These parent advisory members became the principal's biggest supporters.

In that school were several fundamentalist parents (some of whom were on the principal's Advisory Committee at various times) who were concerned that their children were being exposed to books of which they disapproved, and who demanded that the offending literature be removed. The principal clearly stated (backed up by others on the Advisory Committee) that parents had the right to approve what their own child read but did not have the right to decide what other children could read. The Advisory Committee suggested that when a book or film that might cause controversy was to be introduced in class, the teacher would inform the principal, who in turn would call and tell the concerned parents that the material was on display in the office for their review. As a result, this caused potentially confrontational issues to be defused quickly without being aired before district administrators, the school board, or the wider community—and before objecting parents became a disruptive force within the school. The more control these parents felt they had, the more they relaxed—and, ironically, often they didn't even come in to preview the materials.

After this principal left, the Advisory Committee wasn't continued. The next year, some of these same parents angrily confronted the school board at a public meeting about classroom material they deemed inappropriate. Of course, when that happened, the controversy hit the newspapers.

Using Technology to Communicate

As more and more public schools gain access to the latest computer-based communications technology, new avenues for contacting parents present themselves. Besides making the whole communications process easier and faster, this new technology allows schools to select and target a small section of the school populace as easily as a wider audience.

Schools fortunate enough to have access to this advanced technology are putting it to good use. Desktop publishing software enhances the "eye appeal" of such publications as newsletters, flyers, brochures, calendars, and student handbooks. And because these materials are easier to create, schools find that they can be produced more often.

Teachers are able to record, check, and access grades and lesson plans and other important information easily and quickly with computers. The use of e-mail is being extended from school to central office; to homes, businesses, and other schools; and on to the World Wide Web. Homework hotlines to help guide students with assignments have proliferated. Audiotapes and videotapes are particularly effective in reaching parents who can't read. In-house cable television allows districts and schools (and students!) to produce and air their own shows. For creative educators, technology has moved from being an expensive or exotic toy to being a key component of a comprehensive communications strategy.

High-Tech Strategies That Work

A Washington high school has a home page on the Internet, uses e-mail districtwide, has a schoolwide TV network and satellite dish, and makes use of fax connections to all local radio and newspapers.

A Minnesota high school has phones in each classroom allowing teachers easy contact with parents. Their voice mail system allows parents to leave a message for the teacher and receive a reply within a few hours. Many teachers use their voice mail to provide information on homework assignments.

All classrooms at another Minnesota school have telephones, computers, and audio/video access and are networked districtwide. They have developed programs that allow parents with computers to access media materials, contact individual staff members, receive homework information, and check on their children's grades, and attendance records.

A Florida middle school is training parents on the use of personal computers. By joining forces with their neighboring elementary school, the two are able to pool resources for training as both schools move toward more advanced uses of technology.

A Montana high school has access to the fiber optic cable network (Metnet) available in most of Eastern Montana. This provides a full range of interactive conferencing opportunities. They are also a Metnet regional site.

A Mississippi high school has Technology-Discovery Labs that allow students to learn about the latest technology. Parents are invited to tour the labs and view the advances in robotics, biomedical, and other fields.

A Texas elementary school has a video wall in its lobby. By simply touching the screen, a visitor can access a menu of such options as how to join the parent group, information about the third-grade program, the weekly lunch menu, a map of the attendance area and school grounds, and a list of teachers and staff.

An Arizona district has developed a slide-to-video production of district and school highlights for community groups to view. There are shots of campuses, students at work, extracurricular activities, graphs of achievement, a map of attendance areas, and so on.

An Illinois high school has an automated phone call system to publicize events and disseminate pertinent information.

A New York high school finds that with computers, newsletters are produced with greater frequency, their homepage on the Internet provides current district and school information, and e-mail gives greater access to parents and the community without the traditional time limitations.

At an Ohio high school, parents are taught how to use computers and how to use a system that gives parents access by computer to information about the academic progress of their children.

A Seattle elementary school developed a Family Computer Lab to provide opportunities for families who don't have a computer at home. During the late afternoon and early evening hours, the lab is open to parents and students to explore current educational technology together. Sharing computer resources creates a forum for family fun activities and heightens the awareness of the advantages of technology as a tool for teaching and learning.

Using Community Resources to Solve High-Tech Budget Problems

In the race to make computers available to students, many schools have purchased as much hardware and software as their budgets allow. Unfortunately, many have failed to budget for maintenance and repair of all this equipment (and for training as well). If you've worked much with computers, you know they can be quite temperamental—and not easy to fix if you're not an expert. The dreaded "error message" may mean that this particular computer lies dormant in the classroom for months or in a storage room for years. Because schools want as many computers as their money will buy, maintenance is often sacrificed for a few more computers for a few more students. Not a good idea! Donated computers need even more attention because they are usually older—or out of date (which doesn't take too long in the computer field).

Occasional, but regular, computer maintenance and repair are two extremely important areas for which parent or community assistance can be solicited. Within most communities is the technical expertise that could be enlisted for routine computer support and training.

Before Computers

What did we all do before voice mail and telephone answering machines? Remember those "good old days," back when we talked to human beings? Back in the 1980s?

It's mind-boggling to think that just 15 years ago schools were using carbons and dittos and stencils instead of copy machines; 10 years ago, were using typewriters instead of computers; 5 years ago, were using the post office instead of faxing; and a year ago, were using phones instead of e-mail. Internet, here we come!

Note

1. U.S. Department of Education, *Strong families, strong schools: Building community partnerships for learning.* Washington, DC: Government Printing Office, September 1994.

Involvement Evaluation

1. List five new at-home strategies that might work with the parents and families of your school.

_____

_____

_____

_____

_____

2. List five new at-school strategies that you think could be easily implemented at your school.

_____

_____

_____

_____

_____

3. Does your faculty/staff/parent group have a volunteer recruitment mentality? Do they discuss the subject on a regular basis and share creative ideas for increasing involvement? If not, how can you activate such a policy?

_____

_____

_____

_____

4. Walk toward and into your school as if you were a stranger. What is the impression you get of the building?

_____

_____

_____

_____

_____

Of the faculty and staff?

_____

_____

_____

_____

Of the attitude of the students?

_____

_____

_____

_____

5. How do you deal with controversial issues? Has your response been adequate?

_____

_____

_____

_____

6. How many families at your school are on-line? Does your district have a Web site? Does your school have a home page?

_____

_____

_____

_____

If not, can you identify someone in your school or community who could get you started on the Internet?

_____

_____

_____

_____

5 Connecting School and Community

Reaching Your Stakeholders

The Community Schoolhouse

From our nation's beginnings, people viewed the schoolhouse as more than just a place where teachers taught and students learned. It was often a central gathering place for the community at large, a place where both civic meetings and social events were held. As an integral part of the life of their community, people had a strong proprietary interest in their school—it was their schoolhouse and they made good use of it.

Over time, our society has become more mobile, and technology has changed our lives and our lifestyles. We don't sit on our front porches anymore; we sit in front of the TV. Many of us don't even know our neighbors. Membership in civic organizations and service clubs has declined. Discount warehouses threaten neighborhood and locally owned and operated stores. Thanks to answering machines, voice mail, and e-mail, we don't even have to talk to each other face-to-face. Today, many adults have never even set foot in their local school building.

A Disconnected Nation?

Have we as a society become disconnected from one another? Have adults become disconnected from children?

That appears to be the case when people vote for politicians who punish children who happen to have impoverished or irresponsible parents. There is no doubt that welfare needs to be reformed, but to slash key social services and remove the federal assurance of a safety net for children is surely the wrong way to go about it. When we withhold help from children who are vulnerable, in the long run, we only hurt ourselves. To grow into productive, responsible adults, those children need more of our help, not less.

Many adults don't trust young people; in fact, they're afraid of them. A number of politicians plan to "solve" this problem by automatically trying certain 13-year-old lawbreakers as adults. My own state's governor proposes to do away with judges' discretion on whether to try youthful offenders as juveniles or adults and leave that decision up to, of all people, the prosecutor. I hate to think of the effects on society when that 13-year-old comes out of prison 20 years later—or sooner, due to early release from an overcrowded prison system. As one expert puts it, "They will be sicker and slicker than when they went in."

In his 1994 "State of American Education" address, U.S. Secretary of Education Richard Riley asked,

> Is a nation truly connected to its children, child-centered, and committed to their futures when it allows one out of every five children to grow up in poverty and often with violence? . . . If I am troubled by anything, it is this: we seem, as a nation, to be drifting toward a new concept of childhood which says that a child can be brought into this world and allowed to fend for himself or herself. There is a disconnection here that demands our attention—a disconnection so pervasive between adult America and the children of America that we are all losing touch with one another.[1]

Creating a Village

The African proverb "It takes an entire village to raise a child" connects with something deep in our American sensibility as a democratic nation.

As Hillary Rodham Clinton says in her much-discussed book *It Takes a Village and Other Lessons Children Teach Us*, we need to create our own villages, villages that are not necessarily defined on a map but are created from a sense of togetherness. Communities that are connected to their schools and view schools as an investment benefit from an improved neighborhood environment. And such a neighborhood attracts the kind of people willing to "connect," willing to work together for a better future.[2]

One of the greatest challenges facing today's schools and communities is finding ways to create that feeling of "village," a place where we all can feel safe, secure, and welcome. A place where everyone is treated with respect. A place where residents work together to make the village a better place for children and teenagers, for young adults and middle-agers, for active seniors and the elderly.

A low-income area of Phoenix, composed of both young families and retirees, has successfully created a village environment within the city. Thanks to the interest, commitment, and involvement of community, school, and business leaders, the Sunnyslope Village Alliance works to improve overall neighborhood conditions and build pride among residents.

The success of this alliance stems from focusing on local business and education as the heart of the Sunnyslope community. Programs that provide medical treatment for students and families not qualifying for health insurance or assistance programs are provided by a local hospital on elementary school campuses. Local churches offer their facilities for community programs, and the schools serve as a resource and focal point for members of the community. At the same time, Sunnyslope villagers plan special events each year to celebrate their diversity and the history of their community.

Educators have a special obligation to make a conscious and concerted effort to help create this feeling of a village. Our mobile society pushes us in an opposite direction, outward toward the wider world, and our high-tech society pulls us inward toward the isolated and isolating world of cyberspace. We have to stop and remind ourselves that a child's world is small, and this smaller world needs to be loving and nurturing.

Small Schools Encourage Community

It sure helps to build a feeling of community if everyone is known by name. In a 1990 survey by the National Association of Elementary School Principals, 47% of the principals considered a school population of 300 to 500 to be the ideal size, and 38% felt the ideal school should have fewer than 300 pupils.[3]

Needless to say, educators don't always have the ideal situation, so in a large school everyone must work a little harder to build that feeling of community. And even in a small school, community doesn't just happen—it takes planning, organization, action, and communication.

Know Your Neighbors

"Happy families are all alike; unhappy families are unhappy each in their own way."[4]

This observation by Leo Tolstoy is echoed by former Vice President Dan Quayle and psychologist Diane Medved, coauthors of *The American Family: Discovering the Values That Make Us Strong*. Their book focuses on five strong American families—what they're doing right and the legacy they're passing on to their children. As expected, the authors found many similarities in the core values held by these families. They were surprised, however, by one repeated finding.

The authors learned that these parents put great store in a "sense of place" and in staying put. Unlike many Americans who "trade up" to bigger homes in better neighborhoods when their income rises, these families viewed their homes and neighborhoods as the bedrock of their lives. They felt that staying put contributed to a feeling of stability for their children by connecting the whole family to their neighbors and their neighborhood. Even though one of these families lives in close proximity to some of Chicago's toughest sections, the family members feel this connection to their neighbors is so important that they stay put.[5]

Medved, particularly, found this issue intriguing because she had never before heard it discussed within the psychology community.

"It Takes an Entire Village to Raise a Child"

This African proverb has definitely affected our mainstream social consciousness. Of late, it has been in the news more than a little—and perhaps more than we would like. In the space of a few months, this axiom has almost become a cliché. Hardly a week goes by that we don't read about it or hear it discussed on TV or radio.

Not long ago, I read an article by a syndicated columnist who vehemently disagreed with the premise of the Village Proverb. Equating a village with government, the writer castigated Mrs. Clinton for trying to convince the American public to let the "government" raise their children. His own premise: All that is needed to raise a child is a loving family, and this loving family could do a better job if the government would keep its nose out of its business. He went on to say that Hillary and company (i.e., liberals; he used the "L" word a number of times) were trying to come between parents and children.

How sad and how absurd! Am I on the same planet as this man? What does he propose to do about the child whose parents happen not to be loving? What about the child whose parents are missing, in jail, on drugs, or dead? Does he not know that school may be the only positive influence in the lives of some children? Does he even consider foster parents and the help they receive from government agencies?

I think because he hates the messenger his mind is closed to the message. To me, this proverb has nothing to do with politics and everything to do with nurturing children. I may not see eye to eye with Dan Quayle on a number of things, but I certainly recognize the message he was trying to convey about families needing fathers.

Proverbs are proverbs because they express universal truths that withstand the test of time. "It takes an entire village to raise a child" became a proverb long before it was mentioned in the First Lady's book, and it will remain a proverb long after political pundits stop putting their spin on it.

Everyone Has a Stake in Raising a Child

Certainly, a loving family can raise a child, but doesn't it make the job easier if school and community help? It takes a family to love and teach a child, a school to teach and socialize a child, a community to teach and "citizenize" a child.

Forty percent of Americans believe that families need help from their local communities to help raise their children. This proportion rises to 60% when those asked are single parents or those with low incomes.[6]

Working together, home, school, and community have an excellent chance of raising a child to become a caring, informed, responsible adult. All three are needed, because if one falls down on the job, the other two can fill in; if two fall down on the job, the one left still has an opportunity to make a difference. We have to cover ourselves by having as many of these three entities involved as possible. You might call it society's "safety net."

Involving All the Stakeholders

Involving all the stakeholders in a community is the key to creating the feeling of a village. All the stakeholders—citizens, public and private institutions, businesses, and organizations—must have a vision of a better community and participate in its creation.

A suburban elementary school principal in Virginia was able to mobilize a group of principals, teachers, parents, police, social agencies, religious organizations, business people, and so on to meet and discuss basic core values and then to develop common goals for their children, schools, and community.

Educators are uniquely suited and trained to lead this visioning and creating process. The responsibility of running a school automatically makes you a leader in the community. You already have a communication conduit between the school and parents. Use that communication channel and your communication techniques to inform parents about community-wide issues and opportunities.

Cultivating the Media

Expand your channels of communication to cover an even wider audience. Develop your public relations skills and make yourself available for interviews; submit articles, press releases, and editorials to your local newspaper; call in to radio talk shows; address service clubs and community organizations. In short, let people know what your school is doing and what the children of your community need.

> One of our major frustrations is a "misinformed public." It is difficult to communicate to all of our public (parents and community) about what is really going on in our schools. The press is ready and willing to comment on difficulties within the district, yet it is almost impossible to get "good" press items published. (Texas principal, K-5 urban elementary school)

This media negativity is not just a problem in Texas, it's universal. Bad news is usually more exciting than good news, so that's what is printed and broadcast. As an educational leader, you want the public to know that students in your school are excited about learning and are succeeding in the classroom. But is it news? From a reporters's perspective, the school is just doing its job—and that's not news.

Most newspapers have a writer assigned to the education beat. Cultivate a working relationship with that reporter and always be available when he or she calls. Always tell the truth, avoid "no comment" replies, and never say anything off the record. Go out of your way to cooperate and provide information so that a mutual trust level is established. Then when a crisis hits, reporters will more likely be willing to work with you to present a fair story.[7]

Invite reporters to speak to a journalism class or to the PTA or faculty. Encourage reporting of positive stories about youth activities and accomplishments—and then drop a note to thank reporters for positive stories. Suggest highlighting student, school, and community efforts that have taken on violence, drugs, alcohol, and gangs (subjects reporters seem to love to write about). Inform the media about alternative activities to gangs such as opportunities for participation in sports, music, dance, theater, and community service.

Find out filing deadlines for newspapers and television and radio stations in your community. Your school will get better coverage if you respect media time restrictions and release your information accordingly. Yesterday's news doesn't get printed or aired.

Three Communication Principles

In taking advantage of your unique opportunity and your ability to communicate, you must include three specific communication principles[8] in reaching out to members of your community: equality, collaboration, and stewardship.

Equality

For a communications effort to be successful, there must be trust and respect between and among the communications partners. This doesn't mean that all partners must agree on everything. People don't have to agree all the time to form and maintain mutually productive and beneficial relationships. We can agree to disagree and still function successfully together. Equality means that each listens to the other and respects what the other has to contribute. This also does not mean that all partners have to contribute equally. A communications partnership means that all partners bring what they can to the table.

Parents, family, and community partners must understand some of the fundamental principles involved in what a public school is all about. To help their understanding, you must communicate the difference between running schools like a business (which is not good educational policy) and running schools in a businesslike manner (which is absolutely essential if schools are to survive and succeed). For business partners, it also means reminding them that schools have special responsibilities because they are public institutions that are, by definition, open to all who come to them. Public schools cannot cull or discard or say to a child or a family, "You don't meet our quality control standards, so out you go."

For noneducators, being a partner in communications also means understanding that, unlike private enterprise, education must be responsive not just to its clientele and stakeholders but also to the courts, the state legislature, Congress, and any number of other entities that often function as "super" school boards. Creating good noneducator partners requires that educational leaders teach them to recognize these strictures so that they can then communicate the realities of public schools back to their neighbors and associates.

Collaboration

A viable communications plan also means effective collaboration—and this is more crucial now than ever before.

For educators, it means communicating to the entire educational community that public education cannot survive any more with a go-it-alone mentality. The challenges are too great, the time is too short, and the resources are too limited. To succeed, educators must worry less about protecting their "turf" and, instead, spend more time in finding partners to help get the job done.

Expecting that public resources will increase automatically year after year without accountability for the outcomes funded by those resources is a thing of the past. In fact, education funding in many places is declining despite increased student achievement and school accountability.

For parents and community leaders, communicating means careful listening and careful decisions concerning resource allocation where it can do the most good. It also means active salesmanship to enlist other people and other enterprises in the total school-community effort.

Stewardship

A key principle of school-community communications is the simple act of stewardship, that is, protecting what is valuable. What is valuable in this case is the role public schools play in preparing children to become adults, in helping young people to become contributing citizens, and in helping people of all ages prepare for their future.

One of the primary elements of this stewardship component requires both educators and parents to explain, and the private and community sectors to comprehend, what is asked of public schools.

The magnitude of the challenges that confront us as we go about our stewardship responsibilities is enormous. There has never been a time when our schools more closely mirrored society. The stress and strains on families are acted out in children's behavior—and this places a huge burden on schools.

Whose Fault Is It?

Once upon a time, schools were where teachers taught and students learned. And if students didn't learn, it was their own fault. Those days are no longer with us. We're a more enlightened society now, and we know that there are myriad reasons why children can't or don't learn. And we know that it's not always the child's fault.

A child's first teacher is the parent. If that parent doesn't do a good job, it makes the professional educator's job much harder. It's not easy trying to educate the neglected children of noncaring parents, the unruly children of undisciplined parents, the abused children of cruel parents, the hungry children of impoverished parents, or the handicapped children born to drug-addicted mothers. In fact, it's an extremely difficult and time-consuming job. But if schools don't do it, who will?

Placing Blame

Some parents who don't know how to parent blame the school when things go wrong for their child. Someone has called "blaming" the most prevalent disease of the 1990s. It has to be somebody else's fault, regardless of what "it" might be.

I recall an incident in Virginia several years ago in which a seventh-grade boy was accused of dynamiting the custodian's storage shed on New Year's Day. He denied it. But a couple of older neighborhood boys had seen him trying to break into the shed shortly before it was destroyed. Believing the seventh grader to be the culprit, district administrators decided to press charges—not because the storage shed and it's contents were so valuable, but because dynamite had been used. They didn't really have much of a choice because the police were also involved in the case.

At first, the boy's parents suspected that he might be guilty. However, that suspicion didn't last long because their son's denials were so heartfelt and so vehement. When school reconvened after the holidays, the parents tried to prove their son's innocence. The mother spoke with his teacher, the principal, the superintendent, the custodian, and to the boys who claimed to have seen him. By this time, the mother was accusing the witnesses of lying because they didn't "like" her son (although they hadn't known him previously). She was convinced that the authorities didn't really know who had destroyed the storage shed and that her son was being made the scapegoat. She accused his teacher of not liking him because of previous trouble he had caused, and the principal of not believing him because he was new at that school.

The mother was the more aggressive parent in confrontations with the school, but the father backed her in every way. She became more and more enraged because no one would believe in her son's innocence and because the district refused to drop charges against him. As time passed, it became clear that the mother would only be satisfied with complete vindication and an apology. When neither was forthcoming, she hired an attorney and sued. I might add that the boy was basking in all the attention he was getting.

As things calmed down while waiting for a court date, one day (apparently, just out of the blue) the boy confessed that, indeed, he had blown up the storage shed. Because the mother had been complaining about lawyer's fees, her son somehow expected her to thank him for saving her all that money. He was quite surprised when her reaction was not one of gratitude.

Now the mother was as angry at her son as she had been at school officials. But that didn't let them off the hook. Convinced that her son would no longer be treated fairly at that school, she withdrew him and enrolled him in a parochial school—where he lasted about 3 weeks. Then he was back at the former school, in the same class, with the same teacher. There was no other place for him except a juvenile detention center. The mother was invisible for the rest of the year.

Because the boy confessed, this particular case ended after a few months. But there are too many incidents of parents blaming schools and educators for something they did or didn't do, demanding satisfaction, and when they aren't satisfied, suing. Some of these cases that make their way through the court system aren't resolved for years, which takes up a tremendous amount of school and district resources that could be allocated to improving programs and helping students.

I'm not implying that legitimate grievances shouldn't have an opportunity for redress. They should, of course. Rather, I'm speaking of frivolous lawsuits or confrontations that should never even get to that stage—those episodes that can, and should, be resolved by reasonable people taking a reasonable position on what is best for a child.

Many lawsuits are settled out of court because to carry them forward to trial is an expense schools just can't afford. In our litigious society, superintendents almost need an attorney at their elbow. Many large districts have an attorney on staff; smaller districts have one on retainer. The resources of time, money, and personnel devoted to legal issues is appalling—but an unfortunate necessity in this day and age.

Educators Need to Be Mind Readers

Educators have to be mind readers in addition to their other talents. What will satisfy one parent won't satisfy another; what one will accept, another won't.

A high school in the Southwest planned a 5-day ski trip to Colorado beginning the day after Christmas. A permission slip was required from at least one parent of each participant. In signing that paper, the parent agreed that if the child were found with any liquor or drugs in his or her possession, the student would be sent home immediately at his or her own or the parent's expense. The student could not continue to ski with the group, nor could he or she ride back on the bus taking the group home.

The inevitable happened. A senior boy was caught with marijuana. His parents were called and told he was being sent home. The young man bought a bus ticket to the nearest airport, caught a commuter plane and flew home.

The very next year, the same thing occurred. Only this time, the offending substance was liquor. His parents were called, but they did not accept the punishment about to be delivered to their son. They said the trip had been paid for and he was not, under any circumstances, to be sent home early. The teacher-sponsor sent him home anyway.

His parents were at school Monday morning with their attorney demanding censure for the teacher and reimbursement for the boy's trip home. When neither was forthcoming, they threatened to sue. However, in this case they didn't follow through because their lawyer convinced them that the signed permission slip would be difficult to counter. Even the attorney couldn't accept his clients' argument that the purpose of the permission slip was to scare students into following the rules—and not to actually enforce them.

All of this took a couple of months to resolve during which the motives of the teacher-sponsor of the ski trip were called into question. As a result, he decided that, henceforth, he would do his skiing alone. That was the end of ski trips for the ski club—and the club had been taking twice-yearly trips for about 8 years.

What are the messages these parents are telling their sons? The first boy's parents are saying to their son, "Blame yourself. You knew the rules, you broke them, accept the consequences." The second boy's parents are saying, "You knew the rules, you broke them, but you shouldn't have to accept the consequences. Blame the teacher for enforcing the rules and the school for supporting the teacher in that decision."

Different Reactions From Different Parents

Here's another incident of the same problem but different reactions from different parents—and whether to sue or not is less clear.

A high school was sued for $20,000 because of a caption under the yearbook picture of the junior varsity wrestling team. When the proofs came back, the coach was asked to list the boys' names in the order in which they were standing. Five boys who were in the photograph had subsequently quit the team. When the coach filled in the names, as he came to each wrestler who was no longer on the team, instead of putting in their name, he wrote "a quitter." This was not corrected in proofing, and the yearbook was printed and distributed. One of the boys and his family sued.

The school district settled for $10,000. Attorney's fees were saved, and who knows what a jury would have awarded the plaintiff—nothing, or maybe $3,000 or $30,000. Such a thing is not easily predictable. The yearbook staff was certainly negligent and the coach was certainly meanspirited—and the school and district were ultimately responsible for their actions.

What I find most interesting about this case is not what the coach did or that $10,000 was awarded, but that of those five families, only one sued—even after knowing of the settlement. Why didn't the other families cash in when they easily could have? I don't know the answer, but it's intriguing to imagine their reasoning.

In our litigious society, how can school officials know how different parents will react? It's sort of a "damned if you do, damned if you don't" situation. Is the answer to eliminate ski trips and yearbooks and the like? I hope not. But it does mean that school officials

must keep the district's insurance payments up to date and their attorney's number close at hand.

Schools Are a Target

Schools have become a highly visible target and are blamed for
what they do and for what they fail to do. Schools are expected to
correct all manner and number of society's ills. And when they can't,
they are told that they've failed. With personnel and resources
stretched to the limit, it's not possible for educators to help every
child reach his or her full potential. And when they can't, there are
segments in our society ready to cast blame on schools for not doing
the impossible. And for some reason, those screaming the loudest
about the failures of public education always manage, somewhere in
their diatribe, to bring in the phrase "throwing money at schools," as
in "No need to raise taxes and throw more money at education when
teachers aren't doing the job they're paid to do anyway!"

I never quite understand all this "failure of schools" talk when
polls continually show that around 70% (some research puts this figure as high as 90%) of public school parents are satisfied with their
own child's teacher, principal, and school.[9] (The majority of those
who are dissatisfied have children who attend inner-city schools, and
we know that, historically, these schools have not received equitable
funding—which is a whole additional problem in itself.)

At the same time most parents are giving their own child's
school high marks, they rate education in general quite low. Maybe
they've been listening to those critics who constantly denigrate public education and are thinking, "Where there's smoke, there must be
fire; if schools weren't so bad, everybody wouldn't be complaining
so much."

I'm cynical that some of these critics even want to improve
schools. I think their real agenda is to dismantle public education as
we know it and turn a large portion of our nation's schooling over to
the control of private or religious groups.

Once, the public pretty much left education up to the professional educators. But, today, parents want more control over their
children's education, and taxpayers want more control over education, period. That's not bad; in fact, it's good—if the intent is to improve public education.

With private schools seeking vouchers to operate with public
dollars, with charter schools opening across the country in response

to demands from parents for specialized educational programs, with special-interest magnet schools springing up in large urban districts, with home schooling booming—it is obvious that a "one size fits all" approach to education is no longer what the public wants.

Attempts to overcome the many societal problems that manifest themselves in students mean that schools have to become all things to all children. How is this possible? Well, it's not possible—at least not without a great deal of help and a great deal of money.

Accepting Responsibility

Have schools failed or has the partnership between family, school, community, and religious institutions failed? Perhaps it's the latter, because in the past few years schools have been forced to take on additional responsibilities that were once held by the immediate and extended family, the church, and the neighborhood.

If you recall the poll of elementary school principals cited in Chapter 1, 91% felt that one of their top priorities was "accepting and getting staff to accept additional social responsibilities that once belonged in the home, such as good manners and honesty."[10]

A 1994 international survey revealed that 89% of American parents think "families are not taking enough responsibility for the welfare of their children." (Only 29% of Israeli parents believed that families in their country were not taking adequate responsibility for their children.)[11]

As I speak to school groups and education organizations around the country, I often read a litany of the tasks required of teachers today, duties beyond teaching the three Rs. I read it very fast because it is a very long list. In fact, the list is so long it makes one wonder just when a teacher finds time to teach. Invariably, one or more people from the audience come up to me afterward to tell of certain tasks that I've left out. So the list keeps growing.

Remember how principals from across the country described their school populations:

We have an increasing number of at-risk students, students on welfare, and students from single-parent families.

Fifty percent of our students have limited proficiency in English.

We have four emotionally handicapped classes, three trainable mentally handicapped classes, and one language and speech resource class.

Nineteen percent of our students have a primary language other than English (Spanish, Serbian, Portuguese, Haitian Creole, Russian, French, Polish, Vietnamese, Chinese, and three African dialects).

For a student body of 200, the police came to the school over 300 times last year.

We have added several programs for the at-risk students, including an alternative school and a directed studies program.

Seventy-five percent of our students are on free or reduced lunch.

We have a day care program for students who have children of their own.

Thirty-two percent of our 846 students are non-Anglo. The largest ethnic group is Filipino; 173 students from 120 different families speak a language other than English in their homes. A large segment of these families is from Middle Eastern cultures. There are 22 different languages represented at our school.

Understanding what America asks of its public schools and its educators and establishing a partnership role between economic, political, and education leaders has never been more critical. And this requires communication—continuous and continuing communication.

The "Sin of Assumption"

Communicating to your stakeholders just what your community expects of its public schools and its educators has never been more essential. Educators can no longer commit what I call the "sin of assumption." Those who commit this sin just assume that everyone knows what schools are required to do—either by tradition, by certification, or by mandate.

But everyone doesn't know, and won't know, unless you tell them. After all, the school belongs to the community. Your community needs to be aware of all that its schools do. This requires educators to explain—and the private and community sectors to comprehend—the magnitude of the demands placed on public schools today. You can't wait for the media to tell people, or for politicians to tell them, or for the school board to tell them. You have to tell them. And the best way to tell them is to show them. And the best way to show them is to invite them into your school.

Notes

1. Richard W. Riley, "State of American education" address, Georgetown University, Washington, DC, February 15, 1994.

2. Hillary Rodham Clinton, *It takes a village and other lessons children teach us.* New York: Simon & Schuster, 1995.

3. Ernest L. Boyer, *The basic school: A community for learning.* Princeton, NJ: Carnegie Foundation for the Advancement of Teaching, 1995.

4. Count Leo Tolstoy, *Anna Karenina*, Part I, Chap. I.

5. Dan Quayle and Diane Medved, *The American family: Discovering the values that make us strong.* New York: HarperCollins, 1996.

6. Massachusetts Mutual Life Insurance Company, *Mass Mutual Family Values Study.* Springfield, MA: Author, 1989.

7. Carolyn Warner, *Promoting your school: Going beyond PR.* Thousand Oaks, CA: Corwin, 1994.

8. Carolyn Warner, speech before the University of New Mexico Danforth Forum, Albuquerque, NM, February 8, 1996.

9. Stanley M. Elam and Lowell C. Rose, "The 26th annual Phi Delta Kappa/Gallup Poll of the public's attitudes toward the public schools." *Phi Delta Kappan,* September 1994.

10. Fax news service of the National School Public Relations Association, March 22, 1996.

11. "The International Schooling Project, 1994." The Carnegie Foundation for the Advancement of Teaching and the George H. Gallup International Institute. Quoted in *The basic school: A community for learning* by Ernest L. Boyer. Princeton, NJ: Carnegie Foundation for the Advancement of Teaching, 1995.

Involvement Evaluation

1. Other than parents, are any other individual members of the community or community organizations or groups involved with your school? Who and in what way?

_____

_____

_____

_____

2. Do you think the size of your school encourages or discourages involvement? If the answer is negative, how can this be overcome?

_____

_____

_____

_____

3. How do you communicate information about your school to the community? How often? Have you evaluated whether or not your methods of communication are effective?

_____

_____

_____

_____

_____

4. How does your local media treat your school?

_____

_____

_____

_____

Which media outlets cover activities in your district and school?

TV ____ Radio ____ Major newspaper ____ Community edition of newspaper ____

What are the names of the key education reporters in your city or community?

_____

_____

_____

_____

_____

Are you in regular communication with these reporters? If not, why not?

_____

_____

_____

_____

_____

5. Do you have a crisis management plan?

_____

_____

_____

_____

6. List 10 key influential stakeholders or constituencies in your community.

_____

_____

_____

_____

_____

_____

_____

_____

_____

_____

Are they active supporters of your school?

_____

_____

_____

How can you gain their involvement and support?

_____

_____

_____

_____

6 Community Involvement Programs That Work

The Best Ideas From the Best Schools

Benefits of Involvement

If more people would volunteer in schools, they would know what a good job schools are doing. (Teacher Sharon Lewis, Simpson Elementary School, Phoenix, Arizona)

Our school offers many opportunities to be involved in children's education. We realize that the school belongs to the community and can only be strengthened by encouraging and welcoming participation. This belief has been rewarded with the support and dedication of outstanding citizens who have organized volunteer programs, developed assistance services for needy families, rallied community support, and become partners in our school's educational process. (Principal Jeffrey Kane, Forest Meadow Junior High School, Dallas, Texas)

Our school has much more of a feeling of belonging and ownership as a result of family involvement. People feel like this is their school—both kids and parents. We are surrounded by other districts, yet we have a feeling of community among our residents. (Principal Jim Findley, Westside High School, Omaha, Nebraska)

If we are to be effective and to make progress . . . we must unite all school communities: the religious sector, business community, parents, and social agencies. . . . We believe that effective education is an active, ongoing, and meaningful partnership between each school and its community. We believe that all sectors of our community must work together to ensure that students receive their education in a safe, nurturing environment that is respectful of their diverse talents and interests. (*Statement of Beliefs* from 52 State High School Principals of the Year)[1]

Students have given back to their community by volunteering in activities such as "graffiti busters," feeding the homeless, and teaching ESL to immigrant adults. (Principal Perry Sandler, Joseph Pulitzer Intermediate School 145, Jackson Heights, New York)

Community Involvement Strategies

Following are a few of the ways in which schools across the country have been successful in connecting with their communities.

Multiple Community Programs

A high school in Minnesota has developed a community education program, a recreational education program, an adult basic education program, and a school-within-a-school program to reach out and involve the community. They also work cooperatively with community groups to cosponsor on-campus functions such as job fairs, health fairs, and arts fairs. Principal Thomas Blair says, "It definitely helps to have community people work on and visit our campus. Firsthand information never hurts."

Village Recreation Program

A New York high school offers a village recreation program sponsored jointly by the school and the local municipality. They have a community counseling center and a food pantry, and local businesses have formed various partnerships with the school. According to Principal Barbara Ferraro, "All social service agencies work with the school to support families."

Counseling Service and Drug and Alcohol Intervention

A Washington high school has a community organization, El Centro de Pueblo, that provides counseling services for at-risk Hispanic students. Group counseling through an ESD-funded grant also targets at-risk groups such as depressed and suicidal youths and children of blended family groups. In addition, a drug and alcohol interventionist is on site 3 days a week.

Free Immunizations and Vision Screening

An Indiana elementary school, in conjunction with local county health agencies, provides free immunizations for all students.

A Tennessee elementary school provides vision screening by local optometrists, and glasses are given to needy children by the local Lions Club. The school has found that parents whose children have benefited from these services will, in turn, dedicate more time to the school.

After-School YMCA Program

A Memphis elementary school lends its facilities to the YMCA for an after-school program from 3:00 until 6:00. The cafeteria, outside areas, and restrooms are used. Buses bring children from two other schools. About 75 students participate, of which 50 are from the home campus. This school also allows a soccer league to use their grounds during the school year as well as in the summer. The league maintains the grounds during the summer.

Naturalization Ceremony

A Dallas junior high participates in the teaching process through a naturalization ceremony developed and presented as a cooperative effort with teachers. A visiting judge administers the oath to new U.S. citizens. The presentation unites all ninth-grade history students; the band, orchestra, and choir perform; Scouts present the colors; student council officers speak. Local dignitaries, community leaders, and parents attend. The program is televised live to classrooms across the district.

Preschool Partnerships

A district in Ohio has an informal organization for parents of preschoolers. About 300 parents participate, and they are divided into school and then neighborhood groups of about 50 each. In this way, parents get to know and exchange parenting ideas with their neighbors.

Parent Participation Preschool

A parent participation preschool designed for 3- and 4-year-olds is located on the campus of a California elementary school. Last year, 68 youngsters enrolled in this program. Clear lines of communication exist between the preschool and kindergarten teachers.

Educational Games for Preschoolers

A Phoenix elementary district has a part-time, bilingual community liaison who invites parents of preschoolers to participate in a program where they can check out age-appropriate games for home use. She instructs parents in these games, which teach problem solving, recognition skills, and creative thinking through play. Parents complete a card indicating they played the game with their child at least three times that week. When the liaison makes her home visits, she is able to recommend other family social services that may be needed. After a parent and child have participated in the program for a while, games can be checked out from their local school and home visits decrease.

Open Library Night

A Washington middle school has Open Library Night staffed by trained parent volunteers. The community is invited and the library's computers are available for use.

Public Library Programs

The parent reading program at the Houston Public Library is a community-based family literacy project developed with federal library and Title I grant monies. Twice a week for 8 weeks, parents of preschoolers attend adult literacy classes while their children meet in a story hour with children's librarians. This is an excellent opportunity to encourage adult literacy as well as having parents and children share learning experiences.

Bookstore Partnerships

In Howard County, Maryland, a local bookstore has partnered with schools and community members to create an organized opportunity for students to come to the bookstore on a Saturday to purchase books recommended by teachers. The mutual benefit is increased book sales for the store and the encouragement of reading quality, school-endorsed literature for students.

The Community Club

The Community Club, an all-volunteer program in Washington, D.C. that helps students graduate from high school, offers a once-a-week individualized study hall with free tutorial assistance. The members of the Community Club not only help students with their homework but also sponsor workshops on college preparation and financial aid. To encourage high achievement, the Community Club offers a Stay-in-School Scholarship eligible to those who maintain a 2.5 grade point average and attend 80% of the study hall sessions.

Upon graduation, the Community Club offers a small scholarship for each year the student attends college.

Celebrate Education Parade

The city of Gary, Indiana is planning a parade to honor schools and to focus on the importance of education. Cosponsored by the Urban League of Northwest Indiana, they expect over 10,000 participants including representatives from Gary schools, day care providers, members of block clubs, and individuals from the public and private sectors.

Back-to-School Rally

In the fall, the city of Flint, Michigan hosts a large Back-to-School Rally. In the morning are cultural activities and displays of students' work. In the afternoon, there is a parade followed by the Back-to-School Rally. Flint has a strong system of community schools that also participate in this celebration.

New Orleans sponsors a parade, picnic, and Back-to-School Night at a large ballpark in the city.

Day Care

An elementary school in Texas receives support from the local Christian Community Action organization to provide day care for needy children.

Interagency Coalition for Social Services

A Kansas high school is involved with a governmental interagency coalition in the county that meets regularly to see how all agencies can share information and resources to meet the needs of children. The agencies include those that handle social, rehabilitation, and mental health services; the county health department; law enforcement and agencies of the court; and the schools.

Mental Health Partnership

A Montana high school is involved in a partnership with the area's mental health agencies in the development and operation of a commitment facility for emotionally disturbed children.

Critical Incident Team

At an Alaska elementary school, an 8-hour Certified Medic First Aid Class taught by the school nurse is offered to all interested parents. From this group, a Critical Incident Team was organized and trained to deal with natural disasters, a death in the community, or hazardous material incidents. This team has been instrumental in developing policies and procedures for handling incidents of this nature within the school as well as throughout the community. The PTA has been instrumental in the acquisition of first aid supplies, radio equipment, and training for these Critical Incident volunteers.

Crisis Intervention

An Atlanta PTA collects used clothing and organizes and maintains a Clothes Closet where counselors direct families needing clothes and school supplies. It's surprising how many of the clothes come from the school's own lost-and-found collection. They also sponsor food drives and coordinate efforts with local food banks. Parents provide support to the school's crisis intervention teams through training and providing access to community services.

Help From the Clergy

A Wisconsin high school uses local clergy and hospice personnel to help deal with crisis situations in the aftermath of student or teacher deaths.

Service Club Support

At a Minnesota 7-12 high school, the local Lions Club supports the Quest program for seventh- and eighth-grade students (dollars and encouragement) and helps finance inservice training for faculty members. The Rotary Club sponsors scholarships and the school's recognition programs (Student of the Month, Support Staff Member of the Semester, Leadership Maker Award, volunteer awards, etc.). The chamber of commerce assists the Career Development Program with speakers, sponsorship of Career Day, visits to local businesses, and luncheons and gifts. "As these organizations support the school, so do parents support them" (Principal Richard Janezich, Brooklyn Center High School, Minnesota).

Other community groups, both local and national, provide volunteers from their ranks. Two examples are the Junior League, a national organization of young women committed to community service, and OASIS, a national group of active seniors.

The "A Team" Breakfast

Sponsored by the Student Council at a Dallas middle school, students who maintain a grade of A throughout a semester are recognized at a breakfast where prominent citizens speak to the students and their parents. Local restaurants and businesses also offer coupons and discounts to students with high grades.

Discounts at Local Stores

At a Wisconsin high school, DECA students have created credit-card-size cards for discounts at local stores, shops, and businesses.

Recycling

A Texas elementary school is actively involved in a recycling program. One Saturday morning a month, parents and students from a different grade level collect recyclable materials from the community and sell them to a recycling business.

Fun Run

An Oregon elementary school sponsors a Neighborhood Fun Run for all ages.

Books on Tape

At a Minnesota high school, members of the community volunteer as readers of novels for a "books on tape" collection. Certain students find it helpful to listen as they read.

Choir Performances

A North Carolina middle school choir performs at nursing homes throughout the year and at shopping malls at Christmastime.

Open Picture Day for the Community

An Alabama elementary school opens its school picture day to the community. Many parents with preschoolers take advantage of this opportunity, which makes it an even bigger fundraiser for the parent group.

Hire Locals

Whenever possible, an Arizona inner-city district hires local people for staff and aide positions and tries to place them in their own neighborhood school.

Rent Schools to Church Congregations

Many schools in a number of states rent their facilities to church congregations on Sundays.

Community Meetings

Schools all across the country offer rooms and school grounds for afternoon and evening meetings of Scouts, Weight Watchers, homeowner associations, CPR classes, support groups, dog obedience training—or for use by just about any legitimate community group that applies.

Neighborhood Walk

A neighborhood walk through the barrios surrounding a South Texas middle school is held annually to reach out to parents and to help acquaint the faculty with students' neighborhoods. Many students participate in the walk as well. The local TV station covers the walk, focusing on the importance of parent involvement.

Guest Speakers

A Minnesota high school encourages the use of guest speakers. A list of professionals willing to speak to classes is available to teachers. Included on the list are investment advisers, current and former state legislators, a fire department marshal, a college professor, an attorney (who conducts a mock trial for students), a head of a department store, and a meteorologist.

Open Gym

A Texas school has Open Gym several nights a week while school is in session, with extended hours on weekends and during the summer. The city provides someone to supervise. At times the gym is open to all; other times it's reserved for adults or for junior-high- or elementary-age activities; some nights are reserved for volleyball.

Open Public Forum

A Wisconsin high school holds open public forums to present information about the school and community. Political and community leaders are there to answer questions on topics of high interest.

Senior Citizen Volunteers

A California elementary school has an ongoing relationship with a senior center. Twenty seniors work with individual and small groups of children to share their love of reading and writing and to help students experience success in school. The strategy used to develop these relationships requires making personal contact with the seniors, and then continually letting them know how valuable their contributions are to the children and to the school. The volunteers are thanked in person, by letter, and through articles placed in newspapers.

Residents from a nearby retirement community are assisting an Arizona high school to remodel and reopen an observatory to be used by students and community members to study the moon, planets, close-by galaxies, and sunspots.

Churches' Adopt-a-School

Several churches in Memphis have adopted schools—sometimes in their own neighborhood, sometimes in the inner city. Congregation members tutor, mentor, read with students, help in the classroom, offer clerical help, and so on. We are most familiar with businesses adopting schools, but churches often have a mixture of people who are able to volunteer during school hours, whereas businesses often find it difficult to allow their employees to volunteer during working hours.

Golf Tournament

Here is the fundraiser to end all fundraisers. A Texas elementary school in an affluent community organized, with the help of a local corporate sponsor, a golf tournament for parents and friends. They raised $13,000—and they're having another one next year.

Computer Classes

At an Alaska elementary school, parents and community residents are given the opportunity to acquire or upgrade their computer skills. Classes are free of charge, or for a nominal fee college credit can be earned. Computer labs are open two evenings each week and in the mornings before school.

Cable Access Channel

A Kansas high school reaches out into the community through the local cable access channel. They have a student-produced TV program that serves as a source of information.

Kids, Cops, and Pizza Program

At a Texas elementary school, police officers have lunch with the students and answer their questions. It's very informal and very popular.

An elementary school in a Memphis suburb has a Cookies With Cops event.

Police Officer on Campus

An elementary school in Arizona has a uniformed police officer assigned to its campus full- or part-time for the entire school year. The cost is split between the district and the city. "Officer Bill" has an office at school and is very visible on campus. During the year, he visits classrooms to tell the students about his job and answer their questions, and he spends a lot of time on the playground. As the need arises, he visits other schools within the district.

At first, several teachers opposed such an idea. But even the most adamantly opposed now believe that the benefits outweigh their concerns about the presence of a police officer in full uniform (with a gun) on an elementary school campus. The students feel comfortable being around Officer Bill, look up to him, and are not afraid of him; in short, they've learned that the police are the "good guys" and not the "bad guys." Officer Bill is their friend and they know that he is there to help them.

Last year, the officer was approached by an abused child who (along with her mother and siblings) needed to be rescued and removed from the home—which he was able to do. He has made home visits with teachers to neighborhoods where it was not advisable for them to go alone. He has gone by himself to deliver papers to be signed when a parent would not sign them otherwise. In short, the police officer does what is needed at that particular school. The campus is safer, and not one parent has complained.

Building Citizenship

A local businessman has financed a program at an Omaha high school to help students build commitment to their school and community and to heighten their awareness of what it takes to be a good citizen.

Class Community Projects

At a New Jersey elementary school, every class takes on a community project each year. Some of these include cleaning up graffiti, helping in the kindergarten, picking up trash, collecting aluminum cans, having a food drive, helping at an animal shelter, and collecting children's books from neighbors.

Community Service Credit for Students

At a Cleveland high school, all sophomores receive academic credit for spending a half day each week working at a community agency serving such clients as poor or elderly persons. The program coordinator leads a weekly seminar so students can discuss and reflect on their experiences.

At a Minnesota high school, students who serve up to 40 hours of community service qualify for Youth Service credit or Renaissance rewards.

Required Community Service

All student organizations at a Texas high school require a public service component as a requisite for membership. This includes the band, orchestra, drill team, drama group, Future Farmers of America, cheerleaders, National Honor Society, Art Honor Society, business clubs, and athletic clubs.

Two hundred members of the National Honor Society recently spent an entire day with some elderly persons, including escorting them to a local cafeteria for lunch. At Christmas, the Student Council spent a day with and provided gifts for children at a local children's home. The school ROTC unit keeps the roadway litter-free for a half mile on either side of the school.

Student Volunteers

Students at a Texas junior high are involved in volunteer work at Presbyterian Hospital and Retirement Home, the Lake Highlands Recreation Center, and the Dallas Public Library.

Bridges Into Tomorrow's Solutions (BITS)

This Texas high school peer-assistance group works with the seven elementary and two middle schools that feed into it. BITS members serve as big brothers and big sisters to youngsters who need extra time and attention. Li'l BITS, selected by their elementary and middle school teachers and counselors, are kids with difficulties relating to adults, authority, or classmates and who have few social skills, low self-esteem, or just "need a buddy."

VIP Program for At-Risk Students

A Kansas high school has a Very Important Pupils (VIP) program in which at-risk sophomores are given an opportunity to help kindergarten students. Based on the concept that "he who teaches, learns," the VIP students themselves benefit most from the program. And through "caring and sharing," the youngsters make gains in their schoolwork, particularly in reading. These at-risk students are valued by placing them in positions of responsibility as educational helpers and paying them a minimum-wage stipend for their participation in the program. The students spend 2 hours every morning, first learning and preparing, then teaching. Because these high school students are considered academically disadvantaged, they are eligible to receive funding for working with younger students. Earning their own money and the responsibility of a job helps keep these at-risk sophomores in school, improves their self-concept and school citizenship, and increases their school attendance and achievement.

Politically Active Parents

At an Alaska elementary school, parents are encouraged to be active outside the school setting by making presentations to other schools, attending school board meetings, working on legislative affairs, and networking throughout the district. Many are on a first-name basis with school board members and state legislators.

The PTA has become actively involved in any political matters that may potentially affect education. Prior to school board elections, a Candidate Night is held at school for the entire community. School district administrators and state legislators are regularly invited to speak at PTA meetings and provide information on effective lobbying techniques. A legislative chairperson has been added to the PTA board to keep the school staff and parents apprised of all education-related matters being reviewed by the legislature. On-line computer technology is applied to track pending and ongoing legislation.

School Involvement Leads to Neighborhood Involvement

An inner-city neighborhood in Phoenix has experienced a rebirth thanks to neighborhood activism, local school support, and help from the city. Many of the activists first got involved through helping at their child's school. There they met other parents who were interested in improving the neighborhood. There is a natural affinity between neighborhood and school groups because one of the primary goals of neighborhood activists is to make neighborhoods safe for kids to play in.

When their local school was refurbished and repainted, the surrounding neighbors began to do the same to their houses. There was a snowball effect, and the result was increased pride in the whole area. Graffiti has virtually disappeared, and if any reappears, it's immediately painted over. Also, one of the neighbors right across the street has developed a proprietary interest in the school and keeps an eye on school grounds, reporting any suspicious activity to the police.

Volunteers have cleaned up and restored a park that the city had given up on because of vandalism and drug activity. They sought and received a grant to pay for an on-site security guard, and the city has agreed to maintain the park. Parents are no longer afraid for their children to play there, and the basketball court and playground equipment are in steady use. The group has also succeeded in getting one of the city bookmobiles to park permanently nearby.

Another park is planned. The neighborhood group convinced a local business to donate land, a local engineering firm to design the park and community center, a local building supply company to donate supplies, and a local construction firm to serve as project managers. There are a lot of apartments in the surrounding area, and apartment owners have agreed to pay for park security.

Every Saturday night, this community group averages about 75 volunteers who gather for an "antidrug march." With a police escort, several bullhorns and many placards, they parade in front of known crack houses, venting their displeasure at having such activity in their neighborhood. They have caused several crack houses to move or close, and they've also been responsible for getting rid of open solicitation by prostitutes in the vicinity. They work closely with the state's Gang Task Force, as well.

These activists have learned that to solve many of their neighborhood problems, they must seek help beyond the neighborhood. Thus they've become adept lobbyists at the state legislature. They were responsible for getting a law passed in 1996 that will allow slum landlords to be sued if they knowingly rent to criminal elements.

The community feeling created and developed by these activists has spread to include several neighborhoods. For National Neighborhood Night Out in August 1996, over 400 people turned out for a celebration, including the governor. With a core group of only 15, there are over 140 citizens in this community group who can be called on for various activities. And this neighborhood turnaround was all started by one mother who wanted a safe neighborhood for children to play in.

Note

1. *Statement of beliefs.* NASSP/MetLife Education Leaders Symposium. Washington, DC: National Association of Secondary School Principals, October 2, 1995.

Involvement Evaluation

1. List three to five strategies that you do not currently use to connect your school with your community that might be effective.

_____

_____

_____

_____

_____

_____

2. What service clubs are active in your area? Which of these organizations might you be able to involve in your school? How?

_____

_____

_____

_____

_____

_____

3. Are you aware of all of the neighborhood associations within your attendance area? Do you communicate with these groups? How often and on what occasion?

_____

_____

_____

_____

_____

_____

How could you involve neighborhood associations in your school?

_____

_____

_____

_____

_____

4. Does your school have an alumni association? If not, list names of five people who might be interested in helping to organize such a group.

_____

_____

_____

_____

_____

5. List the names of well-known alumni who you think might be interested in helping students or your school. How can each one be contacted?

_____

_____

_____

_____

_____

7 School/Business Partnerships

A Mutually Beneficial Alliance

Why Involve Business?

Two conditions have arisen within the past 15 years that have changed the requirements for young people entering the work world: the globalization of commerce and industry, and the explosive growth of technology. The message is clear: Effective workers need a foundation of learning and workplace know-how. Increasingly, the good jobs will go to people who can put their knowledge to work. Employers must clearly tell educators what students need to know and be able to do to succeed.[1]

> I cannot think of a single more important topic for this country than the education of our citizens and the relationship between work and school. Our biggest challenge is to find the answer to a simple question: "How can a school better prepare its students for a world that is changing faster than ever before?"
>
> Technology is a critical connection between school and the real world. As we move from the Industrial Age to the Knowledge Age, strategic advantage is determined more by ideas and information than by natural resources. Jobs that require the repetition of simple tasks over and over are typically the first targeted for automation and robotics or export to low-wage countries. The jobs that will be in greatest supply are those that require knowledge skills, and these jobs will also command the higher wages.
>
> In this transformation, greater pressure is placed on education, training, and business process as well as on the organizational and communications structures. All education stakeholders—business, community, and policymakers—must meet with educators and develop a plan that will help bring all students to high levels of performance. Whoever expects to lead in the

future must act boldly today. (Michael Spindler, former president and CEO, Apple Computer, Inc.)[2]

We implore the nation's leaders, corporate and business communities, and citizens throughout this country to make a concerted effort to support the need for developing students who are technologically literate. (*Statement of Beliefs* adopted by 52 state Principals of the Year in 1995)[3]

Employers and educators will have to work together to create the kind of educated workforce that can carry the nation into the Information Age. (John L. Clendenin, Chairman of the Board, BellSouth Corporation)[4]

Benefits of School/Business Partnerships

Business and school partnerships help develop a higher understanding among the business community of the difficulties and complexities involved in educating children. Being a small school with limited resources, our adopters have provided the means which enable us to offer a richer, more varied educational experience. And the snacks, prizes, and awards our partners supply for student and classroom incentives help to motivate in academics, citizenship, and attendance. (Principal Janice Sorsby, Balmoral Elementary School, Memphis, Tennessee)

Ways that businesses can support education, schools, and children include the following:

- Becoming family friendly
- Forming partnerships, coalitions, "adopting" schools
- Encouraging employees to volunteer (as tutors, mentors, speakers)
- Participating in school-to-work programs (providing internships, apprenticeships, work-study, and shadowing opportunities for students)
- Offering professional training and summer internships for teachers
- Donating money, supplies, or expertise
- Funding special projects (newsletters, voice mail systems, parenting courses, assemblies)
- Sponsoring career exploration days for students
- Sponsoring business simulation activities in schools
- Making equipment available to students and school staff (computer hardware and software)
- Evidencing support of the educational system to the community

Advantages of a school partnership for business and community include the following:[5]

- Students benefiting from technology, training advancements, and work experience become qualified job applicants.
- A highly skilled and globally competitive workforce makes for a strong, vigorous national economy.
- An improved school system leads to higher property values.
- Employees with families are more likely to stay in an area with good schools.

Securing Partnerships

Partnerships between schools and business/industry are a growing trend. Ten years ago, school partnerships primarily focused on schools' obtaining financial support from local businesses for special projects. Today, educators have to be a lot more creative to obtain active business involvement, and the competition between schools vying for this support is keener. Few businesses today have the discretionary dollars to contribute to education just because "it's a nice thing to do." They are looking for programs that are mutually beneficial and that make use of in-kind resources more than dollars.

Businesses are also looking for programs and activities that can be tied to the company's mission and goals. So before approaching businesses, be sure that you have done your homework and have determined how the school and the business can match objectives. Then you will be in a position to tell the business people in specific terms what you need, how they can help, how it will benefit children, and how it will benefit their business. Your only limitation is your imagination and resourcefulness. The opportunities are out there; they just need to be pursued creatively.

In trying to secure a business partnership and support, consider the following:[6]

- Upper management support is needed from both the business organization's head and the school district superintendent and building principal.
- Whenever possible use the local chamber of commerce. This organization will be able to determine which businesses have interest in working with schools.
- To recruit businesses for partnerships, schools should use families of staff and parents and assess the neighborhood in search of potential partners.

- When a partnership is arranged, exchange informational profiles of the business and the school/district, and give each staff member a copy of the "partner's biography."
- Share the spotlight: Allow displays of partnership activities to be placed in the lobbies of the school and at the business; give special attention to top company officials during school/district activities.

Principal for a Day

One of the surest ways to get business people involved in your school is to develop a Principal for a Day program. Each year, the city of Phoenix has a Principal for a Day program and invites dozens of CEOs, business leaders, and small business owners to spend a day shadowing a public school principal. Several days later, the business people and school administrators are invited to a special luncheon and awards celebration to recognize outstanding school/business partnerships and honor Principal for a Day participants. Many permanent partnerships have resulted from business leaders being exposed through this experience to the challenges facing public schools.

Education Program Director Deborah Dillon says that most business participants are shocked at the physical condition of many public school buildings and astounded by the scope of the principal's job. Because they know principals have a tough and stressful job, initially, many applicants ask to shadow for only half a day. But that's not allowed—it's all or nothing. And what a revelation it turns out to be! After their day's experience, almost all Principals for a Day want to know how they can help the school.

The program in Phoenix has enjoyed such success and is now so popular with business and education leaders that the city is overwhelmed with requests from businesses and schools to participate each year.

Local Business Partnerships

The business community's interest in getting involved in education should be a wake-up call to educators. There is a myriad of expertise and resources available throughout the community—and it should be tapped. Schools need to form alliances and coalitions with business and community groups. We should be inspiring our community to renew its guardianship of our schools and our children. If we want to assure economic prosperity and if we expect America to be a major player in the global economy of the 21st century, education and business must work together. Such a partnership guarantees a bright future. (Arizona business owner)

Following are examples of successful working partnerships between schools and local businesses.

A. B. Green Middle School, Richmond Heights, Missouri

Sunnen Corporation, the only major employer in this small district, sends every sixth grader to a 3-day camp in June. This camp features boating, swimming, and tennis and is the only camp experience most of these children will ever have.

Each quarter, two local banks give $25 U.S. savings bonds to two students from each school in the district. The bond is awarded for outstanding academic achievement and citizenship.

After A. B. Green was the subject of a laudatory article in the local newspaper, the head of one of America's largest corporations requested that his top-management people be allowed to tour the school. He was so impressed that he wrote out a personal check for $5,000 "to support your efforts on behalf of children in your district."

This middle school has become a Caring Community School with social services available on campus for community residents who need housing, jobs, mental health and stress counseling, health care, and so on.

Agua Fria Union High School, Avondale, Arizona

Agua Fria students from sociology classes partner with the Western Avenue Business Association in the town of Avondale and with the city of Glendale in a project to make a mile-and-a-half stretch of the business section attractive to residents and business customers in conjunction with both cities' 50th anniversaries. Students are involved in a long-term, ongoing cleanup and maintenance effort that includes trash pick-up and disposal, recycling, painting, minor construction, and landscaping. In return, businesses have committed to internships, job shadowing, and other career-oriented projects. Students are producing a video, photographic, and written journal of the project.

Agua Fria's Greenhouse/Agriculture project involves an Agriculture Advisory Committee from the community and a gardening group to help develop a greenhouse. A local vegetable farmer is assisting students in planting, growing, and harvesting crops to be sold to local restaurants. Fish farmers are lending their expertise to help students research and raise freshwater fish used in local canal maintenance.

The Future Farmers of America (FFA) chapter works with a nonprofit organization called Wild At Heart to assist in rehabilitation and preservation of birds of prey. Wild At Heart is a two-person family operation dedicated to saving injured or at-risk birds of prey, with particular emphasis on the barn owl and burrowing owl. The school mascot is the Agua Fria Owl, which makes this project all the more relevant. Chapter members will build three hay towers as nesting sites for barn owls ready for rehabilitation release, and they are planning a scientific study of rodent control based on the barn owl population. They will also assist in the capture of burrowing owls in dangerous locations and transplant them to safer areas. The name of this intriguing project is We Give a Hoot.

Andalucia Middle School, Phoenix, Arizona

Table Talk is a program in which seventh- and eighth-grade student writers are given the opportunity to submit poems to be published and displayed at table tents through a community partnership with J.B.'s Restaurants. Poetry table tents are changed monthly to allow as many students as possible the opportunity to experience the rewards of being published writers. Through this partnership, Table Talk gives students authentic reasons to write and brings poetry and a positive image of teens and the school to the community.

Balmoral Elementary School, Memphis, Tennessee

Balmoral has been adopted by three local businesses: Delta Beverage Group, Dobbs Ford, and Goldsmith's Department Store. Among the company donations to the school are a bicycle to be auctioned at a school fundraiser; pizza parties every 6 weeks for students with perfect attendance; refreshments each month to the class with the highest percentage of parents at the PTA meeting; pizza party at the end of the year for students whose parents have a perfect attendance record at PTA meetings; 35 large, rectangular oak tables; chairs for the school office; a TV and VCR for the library; fundraising candy sales at their place of business; $100 for graduation expenses; and $100 to the winner of the sixth-grade Citizenship Award. The bottling company provides Pepsi whenever appropriate occasions arise. There are several Goldsmith's stores in Memphis, but only the one at Hickory Ridge Mall adopted the school, and it displays student artwork regularly.

Because the Memphis City Schools has an Adopt-a-School Coordinator, the principal merely put in a request and the three businesses were matched with the school (over a period of 3 years). Two of the businesses are nearby, but not in the school's attendance area; the third is several miles away.

Brooklyn Center High School, Minnesota

The chamber of commerce supports Brooklyn Center's career development program with speakers and a Career Day. Students visit local businesses and are treated to lunch and gifts.

Champaign Central High School, Illinois

Champaign Central's Business Partnerships Resource Committee works as a clearinghouse for teacher requests for equipment, supplies, speakers, and funding. Teachers write a description of a project along with needed resources, and the committee, with the help of the chamber of commerce, looks for a business sponsor.

The school's Business Partnerships Alumni Committee plans fundraisers and the recruitment of alumni as a source of nonmonetary contributions such as supplies, equipment, and guest speakers.

The Public Relations Committee has prepared a pamphlet of the school's programs and accomplishments for distribution throughout the community, including identifying distinguished alumni. (If contacted, many distinguished or famous alumni are happy to help their old school.)

Cope Middle School, Bossier City, Louisiana

The Cope staff cooperates with the chamber of commerce in an open door policy in which prospective business people who have indicated interest in locating in the area are brought for school tours— sometimes on the spur of the moment. Cope also partners with BellSouth, which sponsors a number of school activities.

Custer County District High School, Miles City, Montana

Custer High works closely with the business community and is active in the local Economic Development Council. A member of the chamber of commerce, they also work with the community's Ministerial Association on a variety of projects.

Eagan High School, Minnesota

Eagan High's principal, along with several business people, formed a nonprofit foundation to provide scholarships for students.

The foundation has also helped to raise money for the fire department, the city recreation department, a senior citizen project, and assisted a citizens' group in completing an ice arena for the town. Many Eagan High parents are a part of the foundation.

Fenway Middle College High School, Boston, Massachusetts

Fenway has a strong school-to-career program built on long-standing collaborations with Boston Children's Hospital, CVS Pharmacies, and the Museum of Science. In each case, integrated curriculum and in-class experiences are paired with on-site work, which culminates in a 6-week senior internship.

Flower Mound Elementary School, Texas

Appleby's Restaurant gives a monthly dinner for Flower Mound's Teacher of the Month. Halliday Realtors gives cash donations to support school activities, Kroger Grocery gives a percentage of sales based on school cards presented when families shop there, The Bus Co. sponsors safety poster contests, and Lewisville Office Supply honors students and teachers with awards.

Forest Meadow Junior High, Dallas, Texas

Forest Meadow sends a letter to the employers of all parents asking that the parent be excused for an all-day conference. These conferences always draw more parents than any nighttime event.

Forest Meadow encourages collaboration with nearby colleges and businesses. History classes participate in Project Business, a Junior Achievement program with local community business leaders. Members of the business community come into the classroom to discuss the operations of specific private enterprises. Students learn what jobs are available, entry-level salaries, corporate benefits, and educational requirements necessary to fill positions at these companies.

Enterprise City (a fictional place) is a program aimed at equipping students to move from the school environment into the workplace. It was originally endowed through corporate donations and continues to receive financial support from local businesses. Students learn how to buy, sell, shop, and manage money; how to maintain and balance checking accounts; how to prepare loan applications for start-up businesses; how to campaign for and elect Enterprise City officials; and how to apply for jobs in banking, journalism, retail, and manufacturing.

Hazel S. Pattison Elementary School, Katy, Texas

The Katy District has a Partners in Education program that is implemented through individual schools. Business Partners send volunteers and give coupons for free items as rewards and incentives for grades, attendance, and manners. Pattison reciprocates with their Business Partners by sending student artwork to be displayed; having students write notes; and inviting partners to the school for programs, to judge poetry contests, to officiate at Field Day, and to participate in celebrations. Business Partners also provide special treats and incentives for the teachers.

Highland Oaks Middle School, Miami, Florida

A group of businesspeople known as the Aventura Marketing Council regularly finds ways to support the school through its Education Committee. In return, students are involved with the business community through work projects, art shows, and performances.

Horn Lake High School, Mississippi

Businesses in the area help in planning and supporting several Horn Like projects, such as sponsorship of DECA and financing their travel to state competitions. Teachers get hands-on training working in local business and industry as part of the inservice training for Tech-Prep.

At an annual Career Day, business leaders meet with students to share information about jobs and job training and also speak to individual classes about their professions.

Joseph Pulitzer Intermediate School 145, Jackson Heights, New York

Pulitzer School recently honored the owners of La Dentente Restaurant with a community award for their contributions to the quality of life in the area and, especially, for their assistance to the school. The owners, two brothers from Haiti, have contributed dinners for students on numerous occasions and were praised for assisting the school in a purely altruistic manner and for being outstanding role models in the community.

Pulitzer has an active Adopt-a-Class program. Assemblyman Joe Crowley has adopted an eighth-grade social studies class for 3 years in a row. The legislator has developed a series of lessons on the law and government, and his monthly visits have fostered mutual admiration. The class is making plans to visit the state capitol in Albany to see Assemblyman Crowley in action.

Another participant in the Adopt-a-Class program is a Pulitzer alumnus who lives in Seattle and works for Microsoft. Autumn Goft-Womack, class of 1977, presented an overview of Microsoft products and career opportunities to the class, and then gave them Windows 95 T-shirts and software (which she helped install). Now Autumn visits with the class technologically through e-mail. The class also has learned to communicate with students around the world.

Linkhorne Elementary School, Lynchburg, Virginia

Local businesses in Lynchburg subsidize a Books for Babies program, which sends a "care package" with a book and other helpful items to each baby born to the family of a Linkhorne student. They also provide funding for a school Express Mail Service, which gives students the experience of running a postal service within the school. NationsBank, Kroger, and McDonald's provide incentives for student achievement with recognition and awards.

B&W Nuclear Technologies (BWNT) supports Linkhorne's foreign language program. Through this program, second and third graders take weekly French classes from a French tutor. Students have traveled to France as part of the French Connection, a student exchange program sponsored by BWNT.

McNeil High School, Austin, Texas

McNeil has a Partners in Education program that involves IBM and other local computer companies that donate computers and equipment for general student use and for specific physics and science class needs. In addition to donations, local companies including Texas Instruments, Radian Corporation, State Farm Insurance, and IBM provide volunteer tutors who help prepare students for state-mandated skills test. These evening tutorials, conducted side by side with McNeil faculty members, also include one-on-one mentoring of at-risk students. McNeil's Booster Clubs are supported by several grocery stores in the area.

Morning Creek Elementary School, San Diego, California

When parents or the company they work for donate a computer to Morning Creek, the Detwiler Foundation donates two matching computers. These computers are adequate to meet school needs because most classrooms don't require cutting edge technology. Often, the school can afford the expenditure for additional memory or software when they can't afford a complete hardware and software package.

Morning Creek has a long-standing partnership with Pardee Construction, a major home builder in the area. Each year, the company selects various school programs to support and fund. They have supported a drug awareness and resistance program for the fifth grade, purchased high-tech equipment for classroom use, matched funds for free distribution of Reading Is Fundamental materials, and purchased a telephone communications program that allows the school to call parents with information about school and community events. A portion of a recent $4,750 grant from Pardee Construction has been used to improve the school's outdoor lighting system so that evening activities can be held in the outdoor picnic area.

Pardee Construction strongly encourages family and community involvement in the school by sponsoring evening family events and the annual family picnic. Their sponsorship of All-American Achievement Day gives the Morning Creek school community and area residents an opportunity to celebrate the good-neighbor spirit that originally attracted them to the area. The school is the beneficiary of a 5K race; the money raised is designated for additional computers and computer upgrades.

Pardee homes are very marketable, in part because of the outstanding reputation of the schools in the area. A picture of Morning Creek graces the company's real estate literature distributed to prospective buyers.

North Star Elementary School, Nikiski, Alaska

The North Star principal attends weekly chamber of commerce meetings and the school makes an annual presentation to the chamber. Businesses have produced a videotape telling about the local schools, which they use in recruiting industry and workers to move to the area.

Parsons High School, Kansas

Parsons has a Renaissance program designed to reward students for their work and continued improvement. The incentives and rewards come through the business, civic, and religious community. They sponsor achievement assemblies and a place in the building where those who participate are recognized. All supporters are given something to display in their business or office that shows they are an active supporter/contributor. Responsibilities are distributed among a wide group of people so that there is a broader range of ideas that support and maintain this program.

Rye Neck High School, Mamaroneck, New York

Business, civic, and religious groups are represented on Rye Neck's school and district Shared Decision Making Teams. The school receives help from business and civic groups in grantwriting opportunities.

Sauk Rapids High School, Minnesota

Through Sauk Rapids' Serve and Work Study/Business Partnerships programs, students volunteer or work off campus. In many instances, they serve up to 40 hours of community service to qualify for Youth Service credit or Renaissance rewards. Business partnerships have led to part-time or summer jobs, apprenticeships, and training for postsecondary work experiences.

Sussex Technical High School, Georgetown, Delaware

Advisory Committees at Sussex provide a vital link between the school and community. Committee members from local businesses recommend new equipment and serve as resources for all technical programs. They donate supplies and equipment, provide scholarships, serve as evaluators of student projects, provide cooperative education placements, conduct field trips, and serve as guest speakers. Involvement has increased to over 200 Advisory Committee members and 120 mentoring firms.

Sussex has developed a partnership with Delaware Technical & Community College as a charter participant in the Delaware Consortium on Technical Preparation. Called Tech Prep, these sequential programs offer rigorous academic and technical studies through which students can earn college credits while still in high school.

Wenatchee High School, Washington

Wenatchee has 60 to 80 parents and community business people who serve on the Advisory Committees for business education, home and family living, electronics, technology and drafting, photo graphics, agriculture, marketing, and health occupations—plus a General Advisory Committee. They also help teachers keep their curriculum up to date with information on current business practices.

Local businesses invite ninth graders for a day of job shadowing and also sponsor school-to-career planning. A yearly Job Fair for summer jobs for juniors and seniors is jointly sponsored by the school and local Rotary Clubs. School personnel are active in community-wide networking with local businesses, law enforcement, health agencies, social service agencies, service organizations, and religious groups.

Westchester Elementary School, Kirkwood, Missouri

Individuals from the McDonnell-Douglas Retirement Club tutor and mentor at Westchester—some for a year or longer. They are outstanding role models and exemplify the desired traits of honesty, responsibility, and courtesy. OASIS, a senior organization, is another dependable group from which Westchester receives volunteers.

A parent who has a landscaping business designed a plan for the school grounds and also initiated and provided the expertise enabling Westchester to win a $14,000-plus grant from the Missouri State Department of Conservation. This money will be used mostly for trees. In addition, the parents have collected almost $4,000 to be used for bushes and plants.

McDonald's underwrites school assemblies. A recent program was presented by a wild bird sanctuary that brought injured rapacious birds for students to observe.

Westchester has a male-role-model program in which men work with small groups, lunch with students, spend time on the playground, help with projects such as building birdhouses, and read to and with students. Some of the men have been in the program for several years.

Ysleta Independent School District, El Paso, Texas

Created in 1992, the Ysleta Education Foundation gives college financial aid to outstanding district graduates. With significant contributions from Young Insurance Agency, Nations Bank, Magnolia Coca-Cola Bottling Company, Ysleta district employees, a former board member, and the present superintendent, the foundation's assets now exceed $200,000.

Adopt-a-School

The Memphis, Tennessee City Schools has one of the most comprehensive and dynamic Adopt-a-School partnerships in the country. Since 1979, they have had a full-time staff person who administers the program; recruits businesses, churches, government agencies, and community organizations for the program; matches adopters with adoptees; conducts training workshops; sends out information and idea sheets to participants; and evaluates partnerships.

When a match is made, the school holds an Adoption Ceremony to make the partnership "official." A formal ceremony lets the adopter see how important the partnership is to the school. At this ceremony, top-ranking officials of the adopting company (as well as the company-to-school liaison) are invited and given a chance to say a few words. A short program informs students, faculty, and staff about the adoption and about the company. One school printed an official announcement and modeled its program (held in the cafeteria) after an old-time radio show, including commercials for Pepsi (the adopter). Snacks were served courtesy of the adopter (who also gave corsages to all the teachers). The next year, for another Adoption Ceremony with a local car dealer, this same school put on a "This Is Your Life, Dobbs Ford" show.

During the school year, company officials are invited to their adopted school periodically to award prizes, plant a tree, judge a pumpkin-carving contest, and so on. These visits help keep the partnership active, reestablish the personal relationship, and keep the Adopt-a-School program a high priority from the top down.

Principals are encouraged to award adopters Certificates of Appreciation and write a letter thanking company officials whenever contributions are made to the school. If individual students or classes receive awards or prizes, they are encouraged to write a thank-you note as well.

A member of the faculty or staff—not the principal; a volunteer teacher, if possible—is designated as school coordinator for each adopter. Each company designates an adopt-a-school liaison as well. Experience has shown that if the two liaisons are able to develop a friendly working relationship, the partnership is more active and the school benefits accordingly.

Experience has also shown that the company employee who is the designated liaison to the school makes a big difference in how much a business helps the school. If the liaison is truly interested in the program, the firm is active and the rewards are great; if the liaison considers the Adopt-a-School program a low priority, that shows as well.

About half the schools in Memphis have more than one adopter. A vocational-technical school has 34 adopters, but in this instance, companies adopt special programs rather than the entire school.

Each September, this citywide district hosts a Kick-Off Breakfast and Workshop for all adopters and adoptees. The principal and teacher-coordinator attend, along with top company officials and their liaison to the school. The 1996 event drew over 1,100 people.

This breakfast is another time for the school to express appreciation to the adopters, as well as a reminder to them that a new school year is beginning with the expectation of a continued active partnership. This half-day workshop offers an opportunity for each partnership team to develop a plan of action for the new year. Principals and school coordinators need to go into this meeting with their school improvement plan in mind, as well as a list of needs.

In late spring, a 6-hour seminar is held, and breakfast and lunch are served. Again, the same partnership teams are invited and this is one more opportunity to thank adopters. There are about 20 to 25 different workshops from which to select, and for the most part, these workshops are put on jointly by adopters and adoptees. Some of the workshops are "Adopt a Friend" (tutoring and mentoring, Rhodes College); "Kraft Klimbers" (academic incentives, Kraft Foods); "Lessons in Leadership" (Federal Express); and "Potpourri of Partnership Activities" (U.S. Postal Service).

Adopt-a-School Coordinator Barbara Russell says that Memphis's program has been a success citywide because of "building-level leadership, strong support from the district, and cooperation between individual schools and the district. Our emphasis is on people first, in-kind donations second; financial contributions are considered an added bonus."

Memphis' Adopt-a-School Goals for 1996-1997

Goal 1. Adopters will assist adoptees in activities or projects that will promote academic achievement of students.

Goal 2. Adopters will assist adoptees in activities or projects that will increase the number of students graduating from high school.

Goal 3. Adopters will assist adoptees in activities or projects to help ensure that students are proficient in math and science and are prepared for college or the world of work.

Goal 4. Adopters will assist adoptees in activities or projects that will help students to be drug free and will help schools offer a disciplined environment conducive to learning.

Goal 5. Adopters will assist adoptees in activities or projects that will help students to be well-rounded individuals.

Memphis's Adopt-a-School Programs (local and citywide)

Variety Clubs' Children's Charity has donated a van for school use for a year. Use of the van has been divided between five inner-city schools located fairly close together. At the end of a year, the donating organization will do an evaluation to see how much the van was used. If used a lot, they will lend it for another year.

The Shelby County Public Defender's office provides speakers to their adopted school on a number of relevant legal topics: "Guns and Consequences of Their Use," "A Criminal Record and Its Negative Effects on Job Searches," "DUI and Its Implications," and "Wrong Time, Wrong Place, Wrong Crowd . . . Felony Murder." Because of their knowledge of the law and the diverse community, these attorneys are popular speakers with both students and teachers.

The St. Jude Liberty Bowl offers Adopt-a-School companies a free ticket to give to their adopted school for every ticket the company purchases. Participating companies receive recognition in the program, and company names are announced over the public address system. This popular college football bowl game is broadcast nationwide; proceeds go to the St. Jude's Children's Hospital in Memphis.

The Memphis and Shelby County Bicentennial Committee has offered to supply iris bulbs (the state flower of Tennessee) to any school whose students, teachers, and adopters agree to plant them. Volunteers from the committee will come to each school to help with the preparation and planting.

In the Safe and Drug Free School competition, Memphis Ice Cream Company provides a Popsicle party for every student and faculty member of the winning elementary school; McDonald's provides prizes for the winning schools; Seessel's Supermarkets gives $100 gift certificates to the 12 most active and outstanding schools in the competition; and Delta Beverage Group provides Pepsi and popcorn for every student and faculty member of the winning schools. CLEO donates yards and yards of red ribbon for every student in the city to wear during Red Ribbon Week of the drug-free program.

The Tennessee Valley Authority (TVA) sponsors a variety of activities with its adopted high school. One of its continuing activities is preparing a dinner for seniors every spring. Memphis is famous for its barbecued pork, so TVA employees set up their equipment and cook the meat on school grounds. It slowly cooks all day long, and as the aroma wafts across campus, students (with great anticipation) want to know if they can have something to eat. The TVA volunteers say, "Sure can, when you graduate!"

The College of Health Sciences and the School of Nursing at Baptist Hospital have adopted individual students. The South Precinct of the Memphis Police Department and the counselors at Harbor House, a halfway house for former drug users, each has adopted an inner-city elementary school and does tutoring and mentoring with at-risk students.

MCI, Burger King, and Delta Beverage provide financial support to pay for Young Astronaut Chapter registration fees and annual awards of $100 each to the most outstanding chapters in competition. This project helps students get excited about math and science through the study of the space program. The Memphis Space Center also provides funds for Young Astronaut Chapter registration and awards, as well as support for the citywide Junior High Math Contest.

One of the most unusual adopters was a group of homeless people who receive food and help from one of the downtown churches. A former policeman, then homeless, organized the group—and it turned out to be quite an experience for all concerned. The purpose was to counsel at-risk junior high students to stay in school. As it turned out, the program consisted mostly of students helping out at the church by serving food to the homeless. As might be expected, the homeless group was transient and not too organized, so that particular partnership only lasted a year.

The local newspaper, the *Commercial Appeal*, provides orientation and training for all teachers who use the Tracking the Tigers program. The University of Memphis Athletic Department provides financial support and curriculum advice for this program whose goal is to spur interest in reading, math, and geography through following college sports.

Cargill Foods has adopted three schools. For at-risk students, they sponsor programs called Girls to Women and Boys to Men. The programs' goals are to instill high standards in academics, citizenship, manners, and dress.

Memphis has 560 adopters, so only a few of the partnership programs are described. Of late, it has become popular to use the word *partnership* instead of *adoption*. Memphis considered changing the name of its program but decided it was too well known by its original name, and "Adopt-a-School" so perfectly describes what their program is all about.

School-to-Work

> Our company decided to get involved in School-to-Work initiatives at a grass-roots level to help prepare a better workforce. All the technology in the world will not compensate for the lack of employee skills. (Noel Ginsburg, president, InterTech Plastics)[7]

Today's School-to-Work programs are trying to knock down the walls between academic education and vocational education. Integrating hands-on learning with academics, students are given the opportunity for participation in work-study programs, internships, and apprenticeships. School-to-work opportunities enable a student to explore potential career fields and learn about the occupational skills and education requirements needed to enter those fields. Businesses, community organizations, and the public sector join with schools to help prepare students to enter the workforce.

Viewing School-to-Work programs as a way to help schools make the transition into the 21st century, 52 State Principals of the Year adopted the following *Statement of Beliefs:*[8]

> We see School-to-Work supporting the needs of students in our community, utilizing community resources, and assisting with high quality academic and career preparation; bringing business people into the school to share with us and to provide opportunities for teachers to work in businesses to get a "real world" perspective; and linking with other community service-based programs.

Jobs for America's Graduates

Jobs for America's Graduates (JAG) is the nation's largest model of school-to-work transition for disadvantaged and at-risk youths. Now operating in nearly 600 high schools throughout the country, the JAG model is locally driven yet must meet a strict set of performance standards established at the national and state levels with input and direction from the business community.

> One of the still largely unwritten standards by which schools are measured is: Can young people get good jobs on leaving school and progress toward a good career? JAG was organized around the proposition that a single individual—the Job Specialist—should take personal responsibility to see to it that young people are well prepared for the jobs in their community and that they pass the only worthwhile test: to secure a job and gain a raise or promotion there within 9 months after leaving school. The secret to JAG's success is accountability. Its 80% positive outcome rate is a direct result of (a) local staff accepting personal accountability for students' graduating from high school

and making the successful transition into work, postsecondary education, or the military, and (b) support from the local business community that has been organized to oversee the program.

Legislative and business support for JAG programs is increasing because it is a very cost-effective way to dramatically reduce social and government costs by helping at-risk young people both complete school and move successfully into the workforce. The strategy makes these young people taxpayers, not tax "users." The message in the polls is clear: The American people are more than willing to invest in cost-effective education and job training programs—if they result in moving people off public subsidies. That is why nine state legislatures and a thousand schools, governmental agencies, and private companies invest in JAG every year. (Ken Smith, president, Jobs for America's Graduates, Inc.)[9]

Delaware. Under Jobs for Delaware Graduates leadership, the Christiana School District has established a work-based learning model at two high schools. Students are targeted in the spring of eighth grade. While working with specialists to attain a set of JAG employability competencies, these special students also receive training in the workplace. In 1994-1995, the first year of the program, 111 students participated in this program and employment was secured for 86 of the older students.

Florida. Another example of success in transitioning students to the workplace includes a program at Turner Technical High School in Miami. Here students can earn a traditional diploma as well as an occupational certificate demonstrating mastery of skills needed for a particular field of work. The students who come to this school do so typically because they have a strong interest in a specific career field. The school has designed its curriculum around a variety of careers: agricultural science, health, finance, public service, television production, industrial technology, and construction.

Maine. The statewide Maine Youth Apprenticeship Program, of which Jobs for Maine Graduates (JMG) is a part, is a 3-year course of study that begins after completion of 10th grade. Working closely with specialists, students choose a curriculum that will help them compete for apprenticeships. Students' schedules are divided between academic and workplace experience.

Lewiston Regional Technical Center operates a JMG school-to-work transition within their program. In addition to students' gaining a skill, the center provides specialists who work directly with young people and provide them skills in time management, résumé writing, leadership and followership skills, and so on.

Nebraska. Omaha junior high school students interested in a construction internship participate in a safety training and career awareness program that includes tours of the workplace and job shadowing at a variety of construction companies. During the second half of the school year, these students participate in a construction project with a local contractor. The Greater Omaha Chamber of Commerce and the Target Omaha Labor Availability Council are both heavily involved in this project.

Ohio. In Columbus, Dayton, and 13 other communities in the state, Jobs for Ohio Graduates programs operate as local, nonprofit organizations with boards of directors drawn from the business community, public sector officials, and interested private citizens. Both employers and board members serve as mentors and give class presentations on the skills needed for their particular work. Business helps provide program funding. These programs often open doors to full-time employment opportunities on graduation.

Oklahoma. The Agricultural Education/Agri-Science Program in Altus is more is more than 50 years old yet has managed to stay on the cutting edge of the highly technological agriculture industry. The diverse nature of agriculture, which includes over 200 career areas, demands a curriculum that explores all aspects of the industry. Altus High's school-to-work transition model uses cooperative teaching, especially among the agriculture, math, English, and science departments, to foster student success in the classroom and a variety of work experiences to connect classroom to career. Recently, students started a pork sausage business owned by student shareholders. In making and selling sausages, students have honed their agriculture and management skills and discovered a real-world motivator—financial success.

Rhode Island. An interesting alternative high school in Providence shows early promising results. Metropolitan Regional Career and Technical Center is designed to allow students to choose their own course of study. Students are allowed to spend their days working at businesses, agencies, or organizations. Although reading, writing, and mathematics are emphasized, academic core courses are not required. Rather, students are encouraged to take courses that fit their career interests. This model is promising because school size is limited to 100 students. This smallness offers the potential for individual attention that large school programs often cannot achieve.

Texas. In 1989, business, civic, and education leaders formed a partnership with the Fort Worth School District in an effort to help restructure the school system. It has now grown to a group of people who represent over 300 firms. Teachers are encouraged to come into the workplace to receive additional training. The school district has coordinated the Fort Worth Project C3 (community, corporations, classrooms) in partnership with the American Business Conference.

The Rip Cord High School Recovery Program in the Ysleta District in El Paso offers classes for students between the ages of 17 and 21 who wish to earn credit toward a high school diploma at an accelerated rate. The classes are small and self-paced and meet four nights a week. The cooperative education class at Rip Cord helps students find suitable jobs, and students are able to earn credit for working. Through the Private Industry Council (PIC), students may qualify for job search help, transportation assistance, child care, and career training after graduation.

South Texas High School for Health Professions in Mercedes, known as "Med High," draws students from 28 school districts in a predominantly Hispanic region marked by high unemployment and low educational achievement. A rigorous curriculum and real-world applications in the classrooms are combined with dynamic work experiences in hospitals, veterinary clinics, dentists' offices, and nursing homes. Staff development is a crucial component, enabling the Med High staff and students to stay on the leading edge of skills for the health professions. The schools' drop-out rate is less than 1%, despite a majority of students who are economically disadvantaged, disabled, or limited-English-proficient. In 1994, of the 124 Med High graduates, 113 attended college.

Corporate and National Partnerships

Following are just a few of the examples of corporations that partner with local districts or that offer help and support to students, schools, and educators nationwide.

Bell Atlantic. Fifty mentors and volunteers from Bell Atlantic help students in a school-to-work initiative (Telecommunications Youth Transitions Program) in Toms River, New Jersey that delivers state-of-the-art high-tech skills in the telecommunications industry. Students acquire entry-level skills for employment, as well as the lifelong learning skills needed to chart a career course for the future.

Through extended day instruction, work-based learning experiences, and a summer work program, students strive to achieve academic competencies that are based on skill standards set by industry. A curriculum called ComLink emphasizes all aspects of the industry, including safety, customer relations, reliability, hand tool training, fiber optics, and computer applications.

CIGNA HealthCare. CIGNA HealthCare of Arizona sponsors an annual Teacher-for-a-Day event. It is one of three special programs sanctioned by the Phoenix Mayor's Office to help link businesses and schools. Designed to bring human resource and personnel specialists from companies throughout the area to elementary, junior, and senior high schools, a company participant is "matched" with a teacher and spends the day helping the teacher with class instruction. The program gives private sector people insight into how and what students are being taught, and it provides a forum for discussion between schools and businesses about how to most effectively and comprehensively equip students for the work world.

Circle K. In a number of schools, Circle K has created realistic ministores that feature many of the standard merchandising elements of a real Circle K store, including a check-out counter with cash registers, uniforms, product displays, simulated products, and fast food offerings. This Learning Center provides students with a unique real-life retail setting through which they can apply valuable basic skills in math, budgeting, reading, art, nutrition, and social behavior.

Coca-Cola. Based on the concept of recognizing outstanding young people who will provide the future leadership of America, the Coca-Cola Scholars Foundation awards college scholarships to high school graduates throughout the 50 states based on their community activities, scholarship, and leadership potential. During their college years, the scholars are given the opportunity to work as interns for the Coca-Cola Foundation, the Coca-Cola Scholars Foundation, and Coca-Cola bottling companies through the country. The Scholars Foundation keeps up with these youngsters as they progress through college and on to their first career employment.

General Motors. General Motors Youth Educational System (GMYES) is an apprenticeship program now established in over 20 locations throughout the country. The impetus for the program was GM Chairman and CEO Jack Smith's concern about a scarcity of qualified automotive technicians. Students interested in being a GMYES student must complete rigorous training in school. In turn, the students are offered apprenticeships by automotive dealerships in their communities. These school/business partnerships are cultivated year round. With strong leadership from General Motors, the program is expected to grow to serve 100 high schools by the year 2000 and expand to train for other employment positions within the automotive industry such as body repair and finance and loan specialists.

GTE Corporation. Communications giant GTE Corporation recognized that its employees are busy and can't always find the time to investigate college options. To help these parents, the company implemented a teleconference to teach employees and their children the ABCs of college planning. Over 1,400 employees and their children participate in this interactive teleconference broadcast live from four major plants to 18 of the company's buildings across the country. The daylong seminar features panels of experts who give presentations and answer questions on college admissions, financial aid, and student life. Everything from how to pay for college to where to send applications is discussed during this seminar.

John Hancock Financial Services. John Hancock offers a Kids-to-Go program at its Boston headquarters that provides daylong supervised activities for employees' school-age children (6-14) during school holidays. The daily cost per child is $20, although $10 scholarships are available to employees whose income is less than $30,000. As many as 50 children can participate each day, and enrollment is based on a first come, first served basis.

Staffed by child care professionals, the curriculum varies by season and by the ages of the children. Children bring their own lunch, and activities include roller skating; bowling; harbor cruises; movies and theater; and visits to museums, zoos, and Red Sox games. Children who participate in the program are covered under the company's umbrella insurance policy.

MetLife. The education program of Metropolitan Life Foundation and Metropolitan Life Insurance Company works primarily with national organizations to address the challenge of preparing students for work and adult responsibilities. Their Partnerships: Arts and the Schools Program enables 12 arts organizations to work with local schools to bring the arts to students. MetLife has published a book that gives parents and other caregivers pointers on teaching children positive alternatives to violent behavior. Surplus computers and office furniture lead the list of in-kind contributions to local school and nonprofit groups. MetLife offices have donated 200 personal computers and over 800 desks, chairs, and other pieces of surplus office furniture.

IMPACT II—The Teachers Network received a $130,000 grant to conduct a Teacher Policy Institute, bringing together 50 New York City public school teachers (MetLife Fellows) to explore major issues that affect teaching and learning in order to challenge status quo thinking about the profession.

MetLife Resources underwrites the MetLife/NASSP State Principal of the Year program aimed at recognizing outstanding principals in middle and secondary schools across the nation. This recognition sends a message to school leaders that "you are important; you make a difference; we need you leading our schools into the 21st century." A 4-day symposium is held every fall in Washington, D.C. to acquaint these principals with current educational issues and the thinking of those in Washington charged with national oversight of education.

Motorola. In 1991, Motorola distributed a publication titled *The Crisis in American Education* to its employees and business associates, as well as to legislators, community leaders, and educators. In his Foreword message, Gary Tooker, vice chairman and CEO, said:

> We are finding it increasingly difficult to find the types of new employees we need in order to continue producing the very best products and services. This difficulty is due in major part to the failure of the kindergarten-through-12th grade education system in developing America's young people to meet the needs of the new workplace. Motorola is making a commitment to become a more responsible customer of the K-12 education system through partnerships with that system at the federal, state, and local levels. Every Motorolan, whether a parent, grandparent, taxpayer, or responsible member of society, is a member of that partnership.[10]

Motorola's slogan for this partnership effort is "Invest in the Ultimate Future Technology—the Mind of a Child."

In 1995, Motorola published another report, *The Role of the Adult in the Life of a Child,* stressing parents' role as teachers, leaders, and partners with education. It provides tips on helping children that relate to the Goals 2000 initiative and the core competencies sought by employees.[11]

Motorola strongly believes in the concept of lifelong learning and has been cited by industry analysts as one of the most ambitious companies in the job-training movement today. The curriculum of

Motorola University is based on specific needs of the company, is strongly linked the company's business strategy, and includes courses on solving performance problems. Motorola extends its training to every employee and in 1995 spent $160 million to deliver a minimum of 40 hours of training to each of its 142,000 employees. The company lays out more than 4% of its payroll for training, far above the 1% average invested by American industry. This has paid off handsomely, because over the past 5 years Motorola has seen annual sales increase by an average of 18% and annual earnings by 26%. Motorola's emphasis on continuous education is a crucial advantage in today's marketplace.

Motorola's goal is to be the global leader in establishing alliances that transform learning systems so that everyone develops his or her maximum potential as a lifelong learner.

Nike. The seventh overall selection in the 1996 NBA draft, Lorenzen Wright, signed a multiyear shoe contract with Nike (even before his first professional game). The deal guarantees footwear for the boys basketball team at the two high schools for which he played. Also included in the deal is a community college women's basketball team coached by his father. Nike was interested in signing Wright because he is playing in Los Angeles (a major shoe market) and because they expect him to be a star player. Wright was only interested in doing business with companies that would provide shoes for those three schools.

Southern California Edison (SCE). Understanding that children's first teachers are their parents, SCE is making an investment in the local community by reaching out to the family to help train parents (7,500 to date) in the East Los Angeles community to participate actively in their children's education. The company supports the Parent Institute for Quality Education, whose goal is to increase student success in school.

Toyota. Education, particularly elementary and secondary schooling, is the main focus of Toyota's philanthropic activities (which exceeded $12 million in 1995). Los Niños School in Tucson is part of their Families for Learning program, a national network of more than 50 centers helping parents work toward a high school equivalency diploma while their children attend preschool under the same roof. Since 1991, the company has partnered with the National Center for Family Literacy to support these centers in 17 cities.

The TAPESTRY Grant program, a partnership between Toyota Motor Sales, U.S.A. and the National Science Teachers Association, awards up to $400,000 a year in grants to science teachers for innovative environmental and physical science projects. For 3 years, Toyota underwrote the Chicago Young Playwrights Festival where winning plays in a playwriting contest for young people were performed.

Teach for America is a teacher recruitment, training, placement, and support program that received a 3-year grant of $300,000 to assist school districts in Los Angeles and Orange Counties in attracting new talent. New college graduates who were not education majors completed a rigorous training program and agreed to a 2-year commitment in an inner-city school. As of January 1994, 778 new teachers had been placed. Of the teachers recruited in 1991, 46% have continued to teach beyond their initial commitment.

U.S. Postal Service. The U.S. Postal Service has implemented its Wee Deliver program in elementary schools around the country to give students the experience of operating their own on-campus mail service.

Family-Friendly Businesses

What do children need? According to Professor David Elkind,

> What is critical is that children feel that they are important enough in their parents' lives that the parents are going to sacrifice something for them. Real quality time is when parents say, "Look, I know I have this meeting but you're more important and I'm going to come to your recital."[12]

Employers need to be supportive of their employees who are parents. The number of enlightened businesses that recognize the need for parents to be actively involved in their children's education is growing. In the past, many businesses—even though they may have partnered with and supported schools; donated money, supplies, or expertise; provided students with training and work experience—haven't really been family friendly.

Many employers have been slow to realize how important it is for parents to be able to take off from work to attend children's conferences, programs, performances, and sporting events. Educators need to join with parents in speaking up and encouraging employers to allow workday time for employees to play a proactive role in their children's education. Because family-friendly businesses are a growing trend in America, it's easier to convince employers to be more flexible in this regard than it once was.

Family-friendly businesses have at least one of the following policies:

- Allow time for employees to get involved with schools
- Allow time for employees to attend their children's programs
- Initiate, implement, and fund specific programs that promote family involvement in education
- Provide resources to employees on parenting skills.[13]

Flextime permits employees to decide, within reason, when to begin and when to end their workday. Such policies allow employees to tailor their work hours to fit in with their family schedule. Flextime is presently an option for 29% of employees in the United States. Another type of flextime, called "lunchtime flex," lets employees work longer hours from start to finish, but allows a longer lunch period to take care of personal business, such as visiting their child at a nearby day care center or at school. Forty percent of U.S. employees now have access to lunchtime flex.[14]

An increasing number of employers offer the option of part-time work or job sharing. Many employees, including 19% of those with young children and 29% of women with young children, say they would happily trade a full-time income for a part-time one to spend more time with their children.[15]

Some employers offer flexible policies specific to education by allowing parents to be late or absent on the first day of school, or by allotting parents a specific number of hours or days off to participate in school activities. Some companies have lenient policies that include not only parents but other employees as well, thus allowing grandparents, other family members, and interested citizens to visit schools—and to volunteer.

Applying for Grants

Because taxpayers and politicians don't seem to be keen on adequately funding education these days, innovative educators must look for other sources. Grants opportunities from foundations, corporations, and government are available at the local, regional, state, and national levels.

To look for grant opportunities:

- Organizations and corporations that award grants usually have a pamphlet or booklet outlining their policies, guidelines, and application procedures—and can be had for the asking by calling or writing to their headquarters.
- Education Funding Research Council, 1-800-876-0226, in Arlington, Virginia publishes a "Grant Makers Directory" that lists many of the education grants available nationwide. Cost for the directory is $50.45.
- Grant information is listed on the Internet (http://fdncenter.org/index.html) by the Foundation Center, a well-organized site that links to Foundation Center libraries, its annual report, a directory of grant makers, trends, data, publications, and more.

There is no question that gathering information and filling out grant applications can be a time-consuming task. But if the information is well organized for the first application, it's not all that difficult to adapt it for other applications. Some school districts receive help from volunteers skilled in grantwriting to help with this task. As state lotteries keep reminding us via TV and billboard ads, "You can't win if you don't play."

Notes

1. *What work requires of schools: A SCANS report for America 2000*. Washington, DC: U.S. Department of Labor, 1991.

2. Michael Spindler speech to the Education Commission of the States, Denver, CO, January 4, 1996.

3. *Statement of beliefs*. NASSP/MetLife Education Leaders Symposium. Washington, DC: National Association of Secondary School Principals, October 2, 1995.

4. *The employee connection: State strategies for building school-to-work partnerships*. Washington, DC: National Governors' Association, 1996.

5. *Public relations strategies for schools and communities* [On-line], July 18, 1996, updated April 6.

6. *Public relations strategies*.

7. *The employee connection*.

8. *Statement of beliefs*.

9. Kenneth M. Smith interview by the American Legislative Exchange Council for *FYI*, the council's journal, Washington, DC, 1996.

10. *The crisis in American education*. Schaumburg, IL: Motorola, 1991.

11. *The role of the adult in the life of a child*. Schaumburg, IL: Motorola, 1995.

12. David Elkind, *Educational Leadership*, April 1996.

13. Families and Work Institute, *Employers, families, and education: Facilitating family involvement in learning*. New York: Author, 1994.

14. Families and Work Institute, *Employers, families, and education.*
15. Families and Work Institute, *Employers, families, and education.*

Involvement Evaluation

1. Identify school needs that can best be met through a school/business partnership.

_____

_____

_____

_____

_____

2. List five businesses within your community that you think would be interested in partnering with your school in some way.

_____

_____

_____

_____

_____

What is the best way to approach each of these businesses—directly or through a third party?

_____

_____

3. Does your local chamber of commerce help in securing partnerships for schools? If not, how can you convince it to make that a part of its agenda?

_____

_____

_____

_____

4. Do you communicate with local business owners or managers to help them make their workplaces and offices family friendly toward your school? If not, list ways that you could communicate to them the importance of being family friendly.

_____

_____

_____

_____

_____

_____

5. What is your district's policy on individual schools applying for grants?

_____

_____

_____

_____

_____

_____

Who in your school or in your community could help your school with grant applications?

_____

_____

_____

_____

_____

_____

8 Unreachable Parents

Reachable Children

Impossible Parents

There are some parents you can reach in the sense that they may volunteer at school, but who you cannot reach on any level of mutual understanding as to what is best for their child or for the school. In other words, that parent doesn't like how a particular teacher runs his or her classroom or how the principal runs the school. And, if that parent is on a mission to "improve" things instead of leaving you in peace to do your job, well, things can get pretty uncomfortable. Everybody in education probably knows a "parent from hell."

This parent knows how to run your school or class better than you do and proceeds to let you know how incompetent you are—or worse, tells your superiors and anyone else who will listen. This parent threatens to sue and causes all kind of havoc at the district and school board level. This parent believes in the innocence or the brilliance of his or her own child when all evidence is to the contrary. If this parent is a volunteer, you know he or she is there to watch your every move, log your every mistake, and then carry tales of horror back to neighbors.

What advice do I have regarding such a parent? Unfortunately, not much, except to develop a thick skin and work on your diplomacy skills. Often this type of parent has a particular problem, cause, or agenda that precedes his or her contact with you and your school. This parent may demand that you solve a problem to his or her satisfaction and absolutely not accept your definition of solving the problem.

The "Parent From Hell"

Following is a story of how two people—one an educator and one a parent—can have diametrically opposed opinions as to what constitutes a solution to a problem.

At an elementary school in a southern state, the PTA president was found to have stolen money from the PTA funds. This was cash collected at a weekend car wash, taken home for safekeeping by the president, but then never turned over the PTA treasury. The exact amount collected at the fundraiser could not be verified, but all agreed that it was around $200.

The other officers of the PTA asked the principal to speak to the president. So the principal confronted the alleged thief, who promptly confessed (citing recent personal financial difficulties) and agreed to pay back the money over a period of time. After several months, very little of the money had been repaid. (It might also be relevant to note that the accused parent had four children in school who were doing fine in both academics and behavior and who knew nothing of their mother's transgression.)

The PTA vice president demanded that the principal bring legal charges against the former president. When the principal declined to do so, the vice president made the principal's life miserable with accusations, calls, and letters to the district office and with attempts to undermine confidence in the principal with other parents. The vice president would not be placated yet did not wish to press charges herself.

The ending of this particular story is that in contacting all of these people to complain about the principal, the parent also couldn't resist adding that she had learned from other parents that there were a number of incompetent principals in the district and that they should all be fired. This accusation sort of branded her as a "nut case."

The woman is like a bulldog and just won't let go. Her children have at least 3 more years before they leave that school for junior high, and she continues to be active in the PTA. Let us hope that the principal's skin is thick and that her diplomacy skills are well honed—for, no doubt, both will be sorely needed.

Supportive Parents

Thank heavens, those parents who cause principals and teachers to have nightmares constitute a minority and are outnumbered many times over by reasonable, cooperative parents—some of whom could even be called an educator's dream.

These are the parents who volunteer, show up on time, and jump right in and help with the activity of the moment without needing a lot of explanation; the ones who respect you even though they know you aren't perfect; the ones who evaluate their own child's ability and behavior realistically; the ones who encourage you and support your efforts because they know you are trying to help their child; the ones you can count on to lend a helping hand whenever a helping hand is needed.

We Work With What We Have

Don't you get sick and tired of hearing that schools fail children? Schools don't fail children. Schools help children! But schools mirror our society, and when society has problems, Surprise! Those problems show up in school. The "Leave It to Beaver" generation is now the "Beavis and Butt-Head" generation. And educators, no matter how good they are or how hard they try, cannot change that fundamental fact.

So we work with what we have. And when we have students whose parents cherish them and nurture them, who are interested in what their children are learning and how they are progressing, we know fortune is smiling on those children. When parents are able to see the child's ability and behavior in realistic terms and are willing, even eager, to communicate and work with teachers for the benefit of that child, we know the chances for that youngster's success in school—and in life—are high.

To repeat: We work with what we have. And when we have children come to us who were born to alcoholic or drug-addicted women, who have been physically or emotionally abused, who have had no love and little attention given them, what do we do? We take them in, we try to build self-esteem, we teach them to wash their hands and tie their shoes, we show them that someone cares about them, we nurture them—and we do all this while teaching them to read, add, protect the environment, and show respect for their classmates. Parents are supposed to do much of this, but if they haven't, schools take on the added responsibility. It's not a choice, it's just what schools do—and have always done.

And when these children reach high school, we are still encouraging them, preparing them for college or the workplace; still trying to help them develop self-discipline and motivation; trying to keep them from dropping out, from getting pregnant, from taking drugs. We succeed more than we fail. But each failure is certainly a loss of human potential, possibly a problem for society, and likely a continuance into the next generation of a dysfunctional family.

You Are Somebody's Inspiration

We all know stories of people who have risen above their origins, who were raised in horrific circumstances but who, through sheer will, overcame any number of obstacles to become successful, well-adjusted adults. We also know the stories of those who weren't able to overcome their own particular difficulties and demons and who ended up in prison or dead. What makes the difference?

I'm not a psychologist and I'm sure every case has unique circumstances, but I believe a common thread in those success stories is that at some point in childhood, that young person made a conscious decision that he or she did not want to follow the example set at home or on the streets and, instead, wanted to follow the example of someone he or she had grown to admire and respect. These children were able to do it because they had a role model, and there's a very good chance that role model was at school.

NBA star Charles Barkley was widely quoted when he said to his young basketball fans, "I am not a role model." After being criticized for that remark, he explained that instead of a sports figure, the better role models for young people are parents, grandparents, teachers, neighbors, coaches. I won't argue with that, but my common sense tells me that all of us are role models whether we want to be or not. We are either a positive role model or a negative role model. And for some children, the only positive role models they come into personal contact with on a day-to-day basis are teachers and school staff.

Unreachable Parents

We like to think that all families encourage their children and work for each succeeding generation to be educated and responsible so that the family name and heritage can be carried forward with pride. Most do, but some don't.

There are always parents who are absolutely unreachable, whom you cannot reach because they have so many problems of their own that they are unable to help their children in any constructive way. Even though we would like to, we know we can't change home situations. And we know that there comes a time when we simply cannot spend any more time and energy trying to reach the unreachable parent.

What do you do in such a case? The same as you've always done. You work with the child. You may have given up on the parent, but never on the child. The child isn't finished yet. Because we can't change home situations, we try to make a difference in the life of a child during our short time with them. They are our children and we succeed with them one child at a time, one day at a time.

Teachers' "Challenge Up"

A. B. Green Middle School in Richmond Heights, Missouri has a program called Challenge Up. At the beginning of the school year, each teacher selects an at-risk student who would benefit from a little extra attention. The teacher tries to form a relationship with that student to let the student know that someone is there who cares about his or her well-being, academic progress, and future—sort of a big brother, big sister, or mentor relationship.

The Challenge Up program has proved to work wonders with at-risk students. The activities that teacher and student do together are both school related and outside activities such as taking in a ball game, hiking, picnicking, fishing, eating at McDonald's, or visiting a museum—sometimes with another Challenge Up pair or sometimes just the two of them.

Challenge Up selectee names are turned in to the principal (who also selects a Challenge Up student each year), and progress reports are written periodically. The mentoring teachers really seem to enjoy comparing notes and exchanging ideas about this program.

A few years ago, one teacher selected for his Challenge Up student a shy boy, quite small for his age and the youngest of nine children. The boy had failed twice and passively refused to do any work in his current classes. His future seemed hopeless. But that year in the Challenge Up program, he received a lot of special attention and slowly began to gain confidence and become a little more outgoing. He also started doing his schoolwork and his homework—or most of it anyway.

Four years later, now grown tall, he came back to A. B. Green to tell the principal and some of his teachers that he had just graduated from high school, the first in his family to do so. And he told them that during his last year at A. B. Green Middle School, he realized that he could graduate from high school if he wanted to, and he hadn't known that before.

Principal's "Challenge Up"

A. B. Green's principal, Arline Kalishman, has worked with a number of Challenge Up students. Here is her story[1] of one she particularly remembers.

> A girl enrolled in the eighth grade at A. B. Green who was completely uncontrollable. Not many days into the school year, she got mad at a teacher and began kicking the wall over and over and over. Needless to say, this activity was disruptive and the girl was sent to the office.
>
> After assessing the situation, I informed the girl that her behavior was completely unacceptable and her mother would be called to come and get her immediately. The girl announced that her mother wouldn't talk to me. I said, "Your mother *will* talk to me." The girl said, "No, she won't." When asked, "Why not?" she said, "My mom's incarcerated and she's only got one phone call a month and you ain't that call." And she was right.
>
> I could get no help from the relative with whom the girl was currently living. What to do? I decided to adopt this girl (figuratively speaking) and become her "mother," to do for her what a caring mother would do. I required that she check in with me every morning before school and every afternoon before going home. I would check her homework assignments and talk with her about school, her classes, her grades, her home, anything she wanted to talk about. I also tutored her. Occasionally, I would treat her to a lunch or early dinner.
>
> As the relationship developed and that girl realized I cared about her and was concerned about her school work and her welfare, her attitude slowly changed. She seemed to want to make me proud of her, to live up to my expectations of her. Her disruptive behavior stopped, the chip on her shoulder disappeared, she no longer fought with classmates, and her school work improved. In fact, she just blossomed!
>
> After that year, the girl moved on to live with another relative and I lost track of her. Did that special attention make a difference in her life? It had to! I know it made a difference in mine.

Kindness and caring, and being a role model and an inspiration, are not easily measurable, so you will never know the full extent of your actions and your influence. All educators have experiences of helping a particular child in a way that you know touched his or her life forever. Probably that child never thanked you. But the influence and the memory remain. It makes both of you have a good feeling, perhaps even bring a smile, when the memory is recalled.

An Educator's Story

This experience[2] happened a few years ago to Pam Stanfield during her first year as a principal. The setting is a rural primary school in Missouri. Stanfield is now principal of Westchester Elementary School in the St. Louis suburb of Kirkwood.

Laughter Is Better Than Lectures

Phreddy first came to my attention when the F-word was written all over the wall in the boys' bathroom. The clue that made us suspect Phreddy: The F-word was spelled with a Ph.

Phreddy was in the second grade and never far away from trouble. He was well known around school for a unique characteristic: He would never ever admit to doing anything wrong. He always denied responsibility, even when caught red-handed.

One morning as Phreddy was walking between buildings, he met a teacher who greeted him with a "Hi, Phreddy." Phreddy said, "Hi" right back. But as they passed each other, Phreddy suddenly turned and gave her a friendly slap on the bottom.

Putting it mildly, this was no longer a happy teacher. After a few choice words to Phreddy, she brought him to my office. I talked with Phreddy; rather, I talked *to* Phreddy. As usual, he was not admitting to anything.

My intended solution to resolving this incident was to get Phreddy to realize the error of his ways and then to have him apologize to the teacher. Well, Phreddy had never apologized for anything in his young life and he wasn't about to start now—and nothing I could say would move him in that direction.

I saw a lot of Phreddy over the next few weeks, and I vowed that I would break through his stubbornness, convince him to accept responsibility for his actions, and get him to apologize. After all, I was a principal and an adult, and he was only a second grader.

So I set about doing just that. And believe me, I had many opportunities to work on him. But he wouldn't give an inch—even through we became pretty good friends. He was a lovable little boy with lots of personality and energy, and he could give a hug that would crush a bear.

One day, he was in serious trouble for fighting, so I decided to take him to his home. I had done this before. He and his mother lived alone outside of town and at some distance from any neighbors. Money was extremely tight and they had no telephone. I didn't know a lot about the family history, but I did know that the mother, overwhelmed with her situation and with Phreddy, always cooperated with the school. More than once she told Phreddy to "mind the principal, because she's your friend and she knows what's best for you." And when she said this, he always gave me one of his big smiles.

As we drove to Phreddy's house, he was sitting in the back seat buckled in. When we arrived, I told him to wait while I spoke with his mother. It was warm in the car so he opened the door. On this particular day, his mother wasn't home, so back I went to the car, told Phreddy I would speak to his mother another time, and closed the car door—or tried to close the car door. Phreddy had played with the lock, making it inoperable, and the door wouldn't stay closed. I couldn't figure out how to fix it, and neither could Phreddy, so I went around to the opposite rear door to examine that lock to determine what needed to be done. While I was fiddling with it, I must have done the same thing Phreddy had done, because now that door wouldn't latch either.

I had an appointment and needed to get back to school, so I told Phreddy to sit in front, reach back and grab the handle and hold the back door closed while we drove. I did the same on my side, holding with one hand and driving with the other—which made perfect sense at the time.

So there we were, headed back to school, and invariably, one or the other of the rear doors flew open whenever we made a turn. Phreddy found these flying doors quite funny and started giggling. I had completely lost my sense of humor.

But as we continued on down the road, the awkwardness and ridiculousness of the situation got to me, because I started laughing, too. And the farther we went, the funnier it got. By the time we drove into the school parking lot, we were a strange sight—two out-of-control people in a car with two out-of-control doors.

But that day Phreddy and I bonded. And the next time I gave him a reason why he should apologize to the teacher he had hit, he said that he understood how she felt and that maybe he should apologize. I asked him if he wanted to do it right then. He said no, he would do it later. I wasn't too hopeful, but before school ended that day, he went by himself and apologized. It wasn't elegant, but it was sincere.

I learned a valuable lesson from Phreddy, and I thank him for teaching it to me so early in my career: "Sometimes laughter works better than lectures."

A Student's Story

Following is a remembrance[3] of Lynda Barry, a cartoonist and writer now living in Evanston, Illinois.

Sanctuary of Schools

I was 7 years old the first time I snuck out of the house in the dark. It was winter and my parents had been fighting all night. They were short on money and long on relatives who kept "temporarily" moving into our house because they had nowhere else to go.

My brother and I were used to giving up our bedroom. We slept on the couch, something we actually liked because it put us that much closer to the light of our lives, our television.

At night when everyone was asleep, we lay on our pillows watching it with the sound off. We watched Steve Allen's mouth moving. We watched Johnny Carson's mouth moving. We watched movies filled with gangsters shooting machine guns into packed rooms, dying soldiers hurling a last grenade and beautiful women crying at windows. Then the sign-off finally came and we tried to sleep.

The morning I snuck out, I woke up filled with a panic about needing to get to school. The sun wasn't quite up yet but my anxiety was so fierce that I just got dressed, walked quietly across the kitchen and let myself out the back door.

It was quiet outside. Stars were still out. Nothing moved and no one was in the street. It was as if someone had turned the sound off on the world.

I walked the alley, breaking thin ice over the puddles with my shoes. I didn't know why I was walking to school in the dark. I didn't think about it. All I knew was a feeling of panic, like the panic that strikes kids when they realize they are lost.

A Dark Outline

That feeling eased the moment I turned the corner and saw the dark outline of my school at the top of the hill. My school was made up of about 15 nondescript portable classrooms set down on a fenced concrete lot in a rundown Seattle neighborhood, but it had the most beautiful view of the Cascade Mountains. You could see them from anywhere on the playfield and you could see them from the windows of my classroom—Room 2.

I walked over to the monkey bars and hooked my arms around the cold metal. I stood for a long time just looking across Rainier Valley. The sky was beginning to whiten and I could hear a few birds.

Easy to Slip Away

In a perfect world my absence at home would not have gone unnoticed. I would have had two parents in a panic to locate me, instead of two parents in a panic to locate an answer to the hard question of survival during a deep financial and emotional crisis.

But in an overcrowded and unhappy home, it's incredibly easy for any child to slip away. The high levels of frustration, depression and anger in my house made my brother and me invisible. We were children with the sound turned off. And for us, as for the steadily increasing number of neglected children in this country, the only place where we could count on being noticed was at school.

"Hey there, young lady. Did you forget to go home last night?" It was Mr. Gunderson, our janitor, whom we all loved. He was nice and he was funny and he was old with white hair, thick glasses and an unbelievable number of keys. I could hear them jingling as he walked across the playfield. I felt incredibly happy to see him.

He let me push his wheeled garbage can between the different portables as he unlocked each room. He let me turn on the lights and raise the window shades and I saw my school slowly come to life. I saw Mrs. Holman, our school secretary, walk into the office without her orange lipstick on yet. She waved.

I saw the fifth-grade teacher, Mr. Cunningham, walking under the breeze-way, eating a hard roll. He waved.

And I saw my teacher, Mrs. Claire LeSane, walking toward us in a red coat and calling my name in a very happy and surprised way, and suddenly my throat got tight and my eyes stung and I ran toward her crying. It was something that surprised both of us.

It's only thinking about it now, 28 years later, that I realize I was crying from relief. I was with my teacher, and in a while I was going to sit at my desk, with my crayons and pencils and books and classmates all around me, and for the next six hours I was going to enjoy a thoroughly secure, warm and stable world. It was a world I absolutely relied on. Without it, I don't know where I would have gone that morning.

Mrs. LeSane asked me what was wrong and when I said, "nothing," she seemingly left it at that. But she asked me if I would carry her purse for her, an honor above all honors, and she asked if I wanted to come into Room 2 early and paint.

Painting's Power

She believed in the natural healing power of painting and drawing for troubled children. In the back of her room there was always a drawing table and an easel with plenty of supplies, and sometimes during the day she would come up to you for what seemed like no good reason and quietly ask if you wanted to go to the back table and "make some pictures for Mrs. LeSane." We all had a chance at it—to sit apart from the class for a while to paint, draw and silently work out impossible problems on 11 × 17 sheets of newsprint.

Drawing came to mean everything to me. At the back table in Room 2, I learned to build myself a life preserver that I could carry into my home.

We all know that a good education system saves lives, but the people of this country are still told that cutting the budget for public schools is necessary, that poor salaries for teachers are all we can manage and that art, music and all creative activities must be the first to go when times are lean.

No Baby-Sitting

Before- and after-school programs are cut and we are told that public schools are not made for baby-sitting children. If parents are neglectful temporarily or permanently, for whatever reason, it's certainly sad, but their unlucky children must fend for themselves. Or slip through the cracks. Or wander in a dark night alone.

We are told in a thousand ways that not only are public schools not important, but that the children who attend them, the children who need them most, are not important either. We leave them to learn from the blind eye of a television, or to the mercy of "a thousand points of light" that can be as far away as stars.

I was lucky. I had Mrs. LeSane. I had Mr. Gunderson. I had an abundance of art supplies. And I had a particular brand of neglect in my home that allowed me to slip away and get to them. But what about the rest of the kids who weren't as lucky? What happened to them?

By the time the bell rang that morning I had finished my drawing and Mrs. LeSane pinned it up on the special bulletin board she reserved for drawings from the back table. It was the same picture I always drew—a sun in the corner of a blue sky over a nice house with flowers all around it.

Mrs. LeSane asked us to please stand, face the flag, place our right hands over our hearts and say the Pledge of Allegiance. Children across the country do it faithfully. I wonder now when the country will face its children and say a pledge right back.

Notes

1. Arline Kalishman, personal communication, August 3, 1996.
2. Pam Stanfield, personal communication, July 20, 1996.
3. Lynda Barry, "Sanctuary of schools." *New York Times Magazine.* Copyright © 1992 by the New York Times Co. Reprinted by permission.

Involvement Evaluation

1. Do you have a method for identifying students who need extra support from school or community personnel? Describe it.

_____

_____

_____

_____

If not, can you suggest methods that might be initiated for this purpose?

_____

_____

_____

_____

If so, what steps do you go through to arrange the extra support that could help these students?

_____

_____

_____

_____

What extra support does your school provide that works best?

_____

_____

_____

_____

_____

2. What organizations or agencies in your community can you turn to for support for "problem" families or students?

_____

_____

_____

_____

_____

3. Would a Challenge Up program be appropriate for your school?

_____

_____

4. Do you have ideas for reaching unreachable parents? Explain.

_____

_____

_____

_____

_____

5. In what way have you helped a particular student that you know made a difference in his or her life?

_____

_____

_____

_____

_____

Do you think that student was aware of the significance it made for him or her? If not, did it matter to you?

_____

_____

_____

_____

_____

Did the student thank you? If not, did it matter to you?

_____

_____

_____

_____

_____

6. Can you think of instances where you learned something important from a student that changed your way of interacting in future similar situations? Explain.

_____

_____

_____

_____

_____

7. All educators have memorable moments of how they helped a student. List some of yours.

_____

_____

_____

_____

_____

CORWIN
PRESS

The Corwin Press logo — a raven striding across an open book — represents the happy union of courage and learning. We are a professional-level publisher of books and journals for K–12 educators, and we are committed to creating and providing resources that embody these qualities. Corwin's motto is "Success for All Learners."